Lavish
LACE

Photography by Amy Setter

Printed in the United States of America

First Printing, 2018

ISBN 978-1-62767-199-6

Versa Press, Inc

800-447-7829

www.versapress.com

CONTENTS

"Did *you* make that?!"

Whenever a knitter wears their knits, deep down we're all waiting for those special words with that particularly gratifying inflection; a mix of incredulity and awe. There's nothing more likely to elicit that response than beautiful, intricate lace.

Even amongst knitters, there's a sort of mystic aura to lace that other knitted garments just don't seem to have. Perhaps it's the storied traditions that stretch from the blustery foothills of the Ural Mountains to the northernmost reaches of the British Isles, or the cipher of charts that seem so unfathomable to the unpracticed. Most likely it comes down to the fact that the look and feel and wonder of an exquisite lace shawl is simply unique.

In this collection, you'll find plenty of projects to awe and inspire, including modern interpretations of the oldest shawl traditions and graceful garments sure to make you swoon. Combining gorgeous stitch patterns with the fibers of surpassing luxury, from softest baby alpaca to pure silk dyed by hand, you'll mostly find yards and yards of some of the loveliest lace likely to come off your needles.

You might even end up asking *yourself,* **"Did *I* make that?"**

CORONET STOLE

by Natalie Servant

FINISHED MEASUREMENTS

Lace Weight:
14" x 62.75"

Fingering Weight:
17.25" x 62.5"

YARN

Lace Weight:
Knit Picks Shadow
(100% Merino Wool; 440 yards/50g):
Vineyard Heather 23657, 2 balls.

Fingering Weight:
Knit Picks Palette
(100% Peruvian Highland Wool; 231
yards/50g): Currant 24564, 4 balls.

Sample is shown in Lace Weight yarn

NEEDLES

Lace Weight:
US 5 (3.75mm) straight or circular
needles, or size to obtain gauge.

Fingering Weight:
US 6 (4mm) straight or circular needles,
or size to obtain gauge.

NOTIONS

Yarn Needle
Stitch Markers
Blocking Pins or Wires

GAUGE

Lace Weight: 22 sts and 34 rows = 4"
over lace patterns, blocked.

Fingering Weight: 18 sts and 27 rows =
4" over lace patterns, blocked**.**

Notes:

This lace stole was inspired by Art Deco designs. The stole starts and ends with tassel-like lace and has a zig-zag lace body.

The Coronet Stole is a rectangular wrap, worked flat from the short end. The repeat section of the charts is worked 3 times per row. The width can be increased by adding additional groups of 24 stitches. Each set of 24 stitches will add 4.25" to the lace weight version, and 5.25" to the fingering weight version.

Only right side rows are included in the charts and instructions. On all wrong side chart rows: K3, P to last 3 sts, K3. When reading the charts, each row is followed from right to left.

Chart 1 (worked flat over 79 sts)

Row 1 (RS): K3, YO, [SSK, (YO, SSK) 2 times, K2, (YO, SSK) 5 times, K2, (YO, SSK) 2 times, YO] 3 times, K2tog, K2.

Row 2 and all WS Rows: K3, P to last 3 sts, K3.

Row 3: K4, [(YO, SSK) 2 times, K4, (YO, SSK) 4 times, K4, (YO, SSK) 2 times] 3 times, K3.

Row 5: Rep Row 1.

Row 7: Rep Row 3.

Row 9: Rep Row 1.

Row 11: K4, [YO, SSK, K7, K2tog, YO, K1] 6 times, K3.

Row 13: K4, [YO, K2tog, K7, SSK, YO, K1] 6 times, K3.

Rows 15-39 RS Rows: Rep Row 13.

Row 41: K3, YO, [SSK, K8, SSK, YO, K1, YO, K2tog, K9, YO] 3 times, K2tog, K2.

Row 43: K4, [YO, SSK, K7, SSK, YO, K1, YO, K2tog, K7, K2tog, YO, K1] 3 times, K3.

Row 45: K3, YO, [SSK, YO, SSK, K6, SSK, YO, K1, YO, K2tog, K6, K2tog, YO, K1, YO] 3 times, K2tog, K2.

Row 47: K4, [(YO, SSK) 2 times, K5, SSK, YO, K1, YO, K2tog, K5, (K2tog, YO) 2 times, K1] 3 times, K3.

Row 49: K4, [K1, (YO, SSK) 2 times, K4, SSK, YO, K1, YO, K2tog, K4, (K2tog, YO) 2 times, K2] 3 times, K3.

Row 51: K4, [K2, (YO, SSK) 2 times, K3, SSK, YO, K1, YO, K2tog, K3, (K2tog, YO) 2 times, K3] 3 times, K3.

Row 53: K4, [K3, (YO, SSK) 2 times, K2, SSK, YO, K1, YO, K2tog, K2, (K2tog, YO) 2 times, K4] 3 times, K3.

Row 55: K3, YO, [SSK, K3, (YO, SSK) 2 times, K1, SSK, YO, K1, YO, K2tog, K1, (K2tog, YO) 2 times, K4, YO] 3 times, K2tog, K2.

Row 57: K4, [YO, SSK, K3, (YO, SSK) 2 times, SSK, YO, K1, YO, K2tog, (K2tog, YO) 2 times, K3, K2tog, YO, K1] 3 times, K3.

Row 59: K3, YO, [SSK, YO, SSK, K3, YO, SSK, YO, Sk2p, YO, K1, YO, Sk2p, YO, K2tog, YO, K3, K2tog, YO, K1, YO] 3 times, K2tog, K2.

Row 61: K4, [(YO, SSK) 2 times, K3, (YO, SSK) 2 times, K1, (K2tog, YO) 2 times, K3, (K2tog, YO) 2 times, K1] 3 times, K3.

Chart 2 (worked flat over 79 sts)

Row 1 (RS): K3, YO, [SSK, (YO, SSK) 2 times, K3, YO, SSK, YO, Sk2p, YO, K2tog, YO, K3, (K2tog, YO) 2 times, K1, YO] 3 times, K2tog, K2.

Row 3: K3, YO, [K2tog, K1, (YO, SSK) 2 times, K3, YO, SSK, YO, K3tog, YO, K3, (K2tog, YO) 2 times, K2, YO] 3 times, K2tog, K2.

Row 5: K3, YO, [K2tog, K2, (YO, SSK) 2 times, K3, YO, Sk2p, YO, K3, (K2tog, YO) 2 times, K3, YO] 3 times, K2tog, K2.

Row 7: K3, YO, [K2tog, K3, (YO, SSK) 2 times, K3, YO, SSK, K2, (K2tog, YO) 2 times, K4, YO] 3 times, K2tog, K2.

Row 9: K3, YO, [K2tog, K2, (YO, SSK) 3 times, K2, K1 TBL, K2, (K2tog, YO) 3 times, K3, YO] 3 times, K2tog, K2.

Row 11: K3, YO, [SSK, K2, YO, K2tog, K1, (YO, SSK) 2 times, K3, (K2tog, YO) 2 times, K1, SSK, YO, K3, YO] 3 times, K2tog, K2.

Row 13: K4, [YO, SSK, K1, YO, K2tog, K2, (YO, SSK) 2 times, K1, (K2tog, YO) 2 times, K2, SSK, YO, K1, K2tog, YO, K1] 3 times, K3.

Row 15: K3, YO, [(SSK, YO) two times, K2tog, K3, YO, SSK, YO, Sk2p, YO, K2tog, YO, K3, SSK, YO, K2tog, YO, K1, YO] 3 times, K2tog, K2.

Row 17: K4, [(YO, SSK) 2 times, K3, (YO, SSK) 2 times, YO, K3tog, YO, K2tog, YO, K3, (K2tog, YO) 2 times, K1] 3 times, K3.

Row 19: K4, [K1, (YO, SSK) 2 times, K2, YO, K2tog, K1, YO, Sk2p, YO, K1, SSK, YO, K2, (K2tog, YO) 2 times, K2] 3 times, K3.

Row 21: K4, [K2, (YO, SSK) 2 times, K1, YO, K2tog, K2, YO, SSK, K1, SSK, YO, K1, (K2tog, YO) 2 times, K3] 3 times, K3.

Row 23: K4, [K3, (YO, SSK) 2 times, YO, K2tog, K2, YO, K2tog, K1, SSK, YO, (K2tog, YO) 2 times, K4] 3 times, K3.

Row 25: K4, [K4, (YO, SSK) 2 times, K3, YO, K2tog, K2, (K2tog, YO) 2 times, K5] 3 times, K3.

Row 27: K4, [K5, (YO, SSK) 2 times, K2, YO, K2tog, K1, (K2tog, YO) 2 times, K6] 3 times, K3.

Row 29: K4, [K6, (YO, SSK) 2 times, K1, YO, K2tog, (K2tog, YO) 2 times, K7] 3 times, K3.

Row 31: K4, [K7, (YO, SSK) 2 times, YO, K3tog, YO, K2tog, YO, K8] 3 times, K3.

Row 33: K4, [K8, YO, SSK, YO, Sk2p, YO, K2tog, YO, K9] 3 times, K3.

Row 35: K3, YO, [SSK, K8, YO, SSK, YO, K3tog, YO, K9, YO] 3 times, K2tog, K2.

Row 37: K4, [YO, SSK, K8, YO, Sk2p, YO, K8, K2tog, YO, K1] 3 times, K3.

Row 39: K3, YO, [SSK, YO, SSK, K8, YO, SSK, K7, K2tog, YO, K1, YO] 3 times, K2tog, K2.

Row 41: K4, [(YO, SSK) 2 times, K7, K1 TBL, K7, (K2tog, YO) 2 times, K1] 3 times, K3.

Row 43: K4, [K1, (YO, SSK) 2 times, K13, (K2tog, YO) 2 times, K2] 3 times, K3.

Row 45: K4, [K2, (YO, SSK) 2 times, K11, (K2tog, YO) 2 times, K3] 3 times, K3.

Row 47: K4, [K3, (YO, SSK) 2 times, K9, (K2tog, YO) 2 times, K4] 3 times, K3.

Row 49: K3, YO, [SSK, K3, (YO, SSK) 2 times, K7, (K2tog, YO) 2 times, K4, YO] 3 times, K2tog, K2.

Row 51: K4, [YO, SSK, K3, (YO, SSK) 2 times, K5, (K2tog, YO) 2 times, K3, K2tog, YO, K1] 3 times, K3.

Row 53: K3, YO, [SSK, YO, SSK, K3, (YO, SSK) 2 times, K3, (K2tog, YO) 2 times, K3, K2tog, YO, K1, YO] 3 times, K2tog, K2.

Row 55: K4, [(YO, SSK) 2 times, K3, (YO, SSK) 2 times, K1, (K2tog, YO) 2 times, K3, (K2tog, YO) 2 times, K1] 3 times, K3.
Rep Rows 1-55 for pattern.

Chart 3 (worked flat over 79 sts)

Row 1 (RS): K3, YO, [SSK, (YO, SSK) 2 times, K3, YO, SSK, YO, Sk2p, YO, K2tog, YO, K3, (K2tog, YO) 2 times, K1, YO] 3 times, K2tog, K2.

Row 3: K3, YO, [K2tog, K1, (YO, SSK) 2 times, K3, YO, SSK, YO, K3tog, YO, K3, (K2tog, YO) 2 times, K2, YO] 3 times, K2tog, K2.

Row 5: K3, YO, [K2tog, K2, (YO, SSK) 2 times, K3, YO, Sk2p, YO, K3, (K2tog, YO) 2 times, K3, YO] 3 times, K2tog, K2.

Row 7: K3, YO, [K2tog, K3, (YO, SSK) 2 times, K3, YO, SSK, K2, (K2tog, YO) 2 times, K4, YO] 3 times, K2tog, K2.

Row 9: K3, YO, [K2tog, K2, (YO, SSK) 3 times, K2, K1 TBL, K2, (K2tog, YO) 3 times, K3, YO] 3 times, K2tog, K2.

Row 11: K3, YO, [SSK, K2, YO, K2tog, K1, (YO, SSK) 2 times, K3, (K2tog, YO) 2 times, K1, SSK, YO, K3, YO] 3 times, K2tog, K2.

Row 13: K4, [YO, SSK, K1, YO, K2tog, K2, (YO, SSK) 2 times, K1, (K2tog, YO) 2 times, K2, SSK, YO, K1, K2tog, YO, K1] 3 times, K3.

Row 15: K3, YO, [(SSK, YO) two times, K2tog, K3, YO, SSK, YO, Sk2p, YO, K2tog, YO, K3, SSK, YO, K2tog, YO, K1, YO] 3 times, K2tog, K2.

Row 17: K4, [(YO, SSK) 2 times, K3, (YO, SSK) 2 times, YO, K3tog, YO, K2tog, YO, K3, (K2tog, YO) 2 times, K1] 3 times, K3.

Row 19: K4, [K1, (YO, SSK) 2 times, K2, YO, K2tog, K1, YO, Sk2p, YO, K1, SSK, YO, K2, (K2tog, YO) 2 times, K2] K3.

Row 21: K4, [(YO, SSK) 3 times, K1, YO, K2tog, K2, YO, SSK, K1, SSK, YO, K1, (K2tog, YO) 3 times, K1] 3 times, K3.

Row 23: K4, [YO, K2tog, K1, (YO, SSK) 2 times, YO, K2tog, K2, YO, K2tog, K1, SSK, YO, (K2tog, YO) 2 times, K1, SSK, YO, K1] 3 times, K3.

Row 25: K4, [YO, K2tog, K2, (YO, SSK) 2 times, K3, YO, K2tog, K2, (K2tog, YO) 2 times, K2, SSK, YO, K1] 3 times, K3.

Row 27: K4, [YO, K2tog, K3, (YO, SSK) 2 times, K2, YO, K2tog, K1, (K2tog, YO) 2 times, K3, SSK, YO, K1] 3 times, K3.

Row 29: K4, [YO, K2tog, K4, (YO, SSK) 2 times, K1, YO, K2tog, (K2tog, YO) 2 times, K4, SSK, YO, K1] 3 times, K3.

Row 31: K4, [YO, K2tog, K5, (YO, SSK) 2 times, YO, K3tog, YO, K2tog, YO, K5, SSK, YO, K1] 3 times, K3.

Row 33: K4, [YO, K2tog, K6, YO, SSK, YO, Sk2p, YO, K2tog, YO, K6, SSK, YO, K1] 3 times, K3.

Row 35: K4, [YO, K2tog, K7, YO, SSK, YO, K3tog, YO, K7, SSK, YO, K1] 3 times, K3.

Row 37: K4, [YO, K2tog, K8, YO, Sk2p, YO, K8, SSK, YO, K1] 3 times, K3.

Row 39: K4, [YO, K2tog, K9, YO, SSK, K8, SSK, YO, K1] 3 times, K3.

Row 41: K4, [YO, K2tog, K7, K2tog, YO, K1, YO, SSK, K7, SSK, YO, K1] 3 times, K3.

Row 43: K4, [YO, K2tog, K7, SSK, YO, K1] 6 times, K3.

Rows 45-69 RS Rows: Rep Row 43.

Row 71: K3, YO, [SSK, (YO, SSK) 2 times, K2, (YO, SSK) 5 times, K2, (YO, SSK) 2 times, YO] 3 times, K2tog, K2.

Row 73: K4, [(YO, SSK) 2 times, K4, (YO, SSK) 4 times, K4, (YO, SSK) 2 times] 3 times, K3.

Row 75: Rep Row 71.

Row 77: Rep Row 73.

Row 79: Rep Row 71.

DIRECTIONS

Loosely CO 79 sts.

Knit 6 rows.

Work Chart 1. The repeat area is worked 3 times per row.

Work Chart 2 seven times in lace weight, or five times in fingering weight.

Work Chart 3, ending on Row 79.

Knit 6 rows.

BO loosely.

Finishing

Weave in ends, wash, and block to measurements using blocking wires or pins.

Chart 1

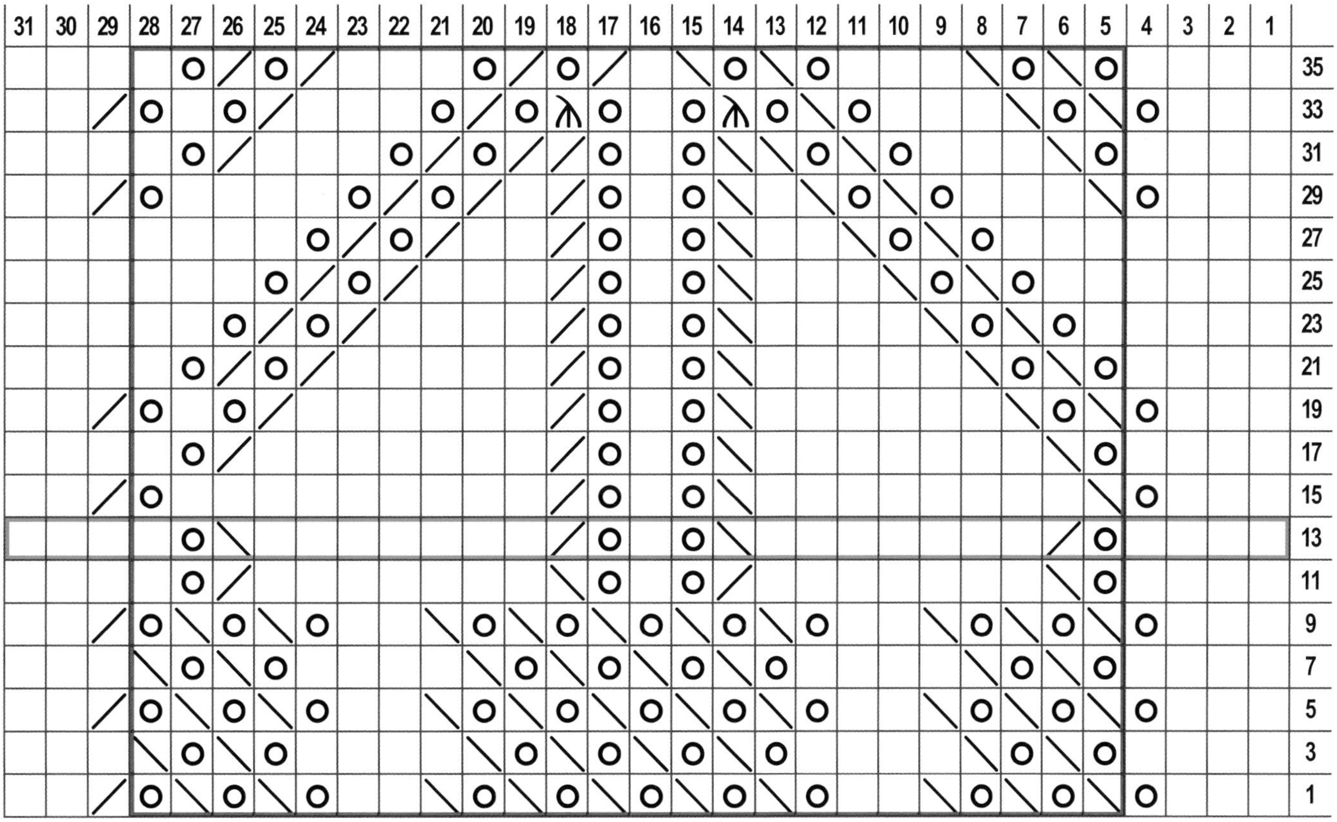

Legend

☐ **K**
Knit stitch

⊙ **YO**
Yarn Over

B **Knit TBL**
Knit stitch through back loop.

╱ **K2tog**
Knit 2 stitches together as 1 stitch.

╲ **SSK**
Slip 1 stitch as if to knit. Slip another stitch as if to knit. Insert LH needle into front of these 2 stitches and knit them together.

⋏ **sl1 K2tog PSSO (SK2P)**
Slip 1 stitch. K2tog then pass the slipped stitch over.

╱ **K3tog**
Knit three stitches together as one.

☐ **Pattern Repeat**

☐ **Chart 1 Repeat**
On Chart 1 work Rows 13-14 a total of 14 times.

☐ **Chart 3 Repeat**
On Chart 3 work Rows 43-44 a total of 14 times.

Chart 2

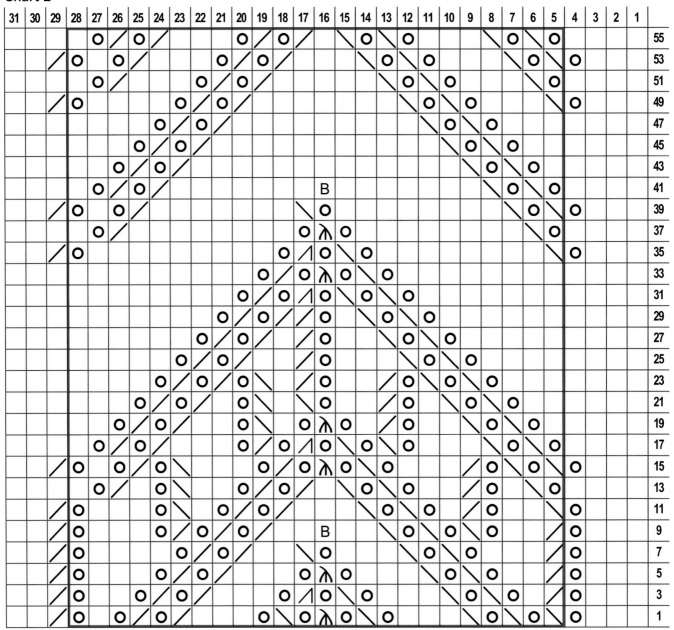

Chart 3

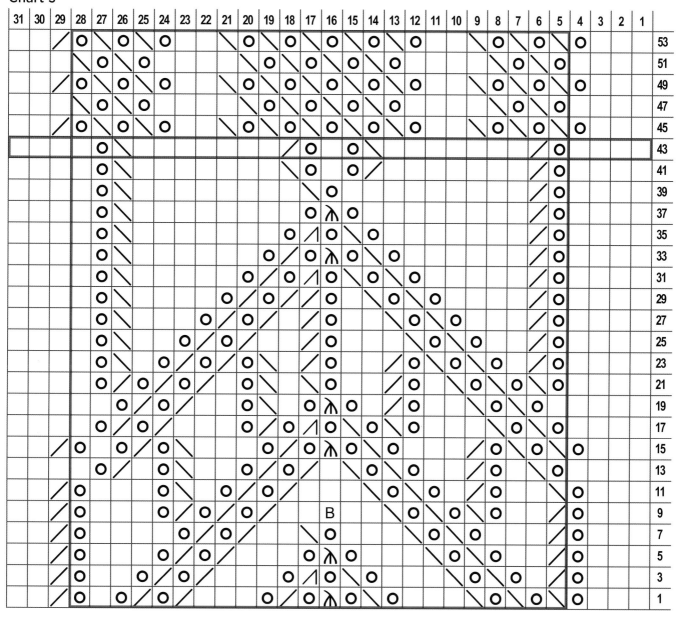

CYMOPOLEIA

by Claire Slade

FINISHED MEASUREMENTS
84" diameter

YARN
Knit Picks Alpaca Cloud Lace Yarn
(100% Baby Alpaca; 440 yards/50g):
Hugh 26770, 5 skeins

NEEDLES
US 6 (4mm) DPNs, 16", 24" and 32"
circular needles, or size to obtain gauge.

NOTIONS
Yarn Needle
9 Stitch Markers
Blocking Pins

GAUGE
24 sts and 24 rows = 4" over Rippling
Water Lace Patterns, aggressively
blocked. (Gauge for this project is
approximate but will affect finished size
and yardage requirements).

Notes:

Inspired by Greek sea mythology, Cymopoleia is named after the daughter of Poseidon, the goddess of violent storms. The three sections of the shawl are reminiscent of the sea; the center starts with a spiraling fishing net, then the lace changes to rippling water, finishing with the waves crashing on the shore as detailed in the outer edging.

This large circular shawl is knit in the round from the center out; once the main body of the shawl is complete a knitted on border is added. When only odd numbered chart rows are shown, refer to the pattern for even row number directions. When working charts flat, read the RS rows (odd numbers) from right to left, and WS rows (even numbers) from left to right. When working charts in the rnd, follow all chart rows from right to left, reading them as RS rows.

A tutorial for the Cable Cast On can be found here: http://tutorials.knitpicks.com/cabled-cast-on/

DIRECTIONS

CO 9 sts onto DPN's and join to work in the rnd being careful not to twist. As sts are increased, change to progressively longer circular needles as needed.

Setup Section

Rnd 1: *YO, K1; rep from * to end. 18 sts.
Rnd 2: *K2, PM; rep from * to end. There will be 9 sections.
Rnd 3: *YO, K to M, SM; rep from * to end. 9 sts inc, 1 in each section.
Rnd 4: K.
Rnds 5-8: Rep Rnds 3-4 twice. 45 sts, 5 sts in each section.
Rnd 9: *YO, K2, YO, K2tog, K1, SM; rep from * to end. 54 sts.
Rnd 10: K.
Rnd 11: *YO, K3, YO, K2tog, K1, SM; rep from * to end. 63 sts.
Rnd 12: K.
Rnd 13: *YO, K2, (YO, K2tog) twice, K1, SM; rep from * to end. 72 sts, 8 sts in each section.
Rnd 14: K.

Fishing Net Lace Section

Rnd 1: **YO, K3, *YO, K2tog; rep from * to 1 st before M, K1, SM; rep from ** to end. 9 sts inc.
Rnd 2: K.
Rnd 3: **YO, K2, *YO, K2tog; rep from * to 1 st, before M, K1, SM; rep from ** to end. 9 sts inc.
Rnd 4: K.
Rep Rnds 1-4 seventeen more times, until you have 396 sts, 44 sts in each section.

Rippling Water Lace Section

All odd numbered rnds are worked as follows: *Work chart to marker repeating the red box section, SM; rep from * to end. All even numbered rnds (which are not shown on the charts) are knit.

Work Rnds 1-26 of Chart A once. 513 sts, 57 sts in each section.
Work Rnds 1-32 of Chart B once. 657 sts, 73 sts in each section.
Work Rnds 1-26 of Chart C once. On the final rnd remove all markers except the one at the beginning of the rnd. 765 sts, 85 sts in each section.
Work Rnds 1-5 of Chart D once. At the end of Rnd 4 move the beginning of rnd marker back 1 st.
Next 5 Rnds: K, increasing 3sts evenly on Rnd 2. 768 sts. Leave all sts on circular needle, do not break yarn.

Crashing Waves Edging

The edging is knit flat back and forth. After the edging sts have been CO next to the shawl sts, the edging is worked from the chart. At the end of each RS chart row, the last st of the edging is knit together with the next live shawl st TBL and the work is then turned to the WS. On the WS row the first st is always slipped P-wise.

With RS facing CO 19 sts using the Cable Cast On next to the live shawl sts.
Rep Rows 1-16 of Edging Chart until all shawl sts have been worked.
BO all sts.

Finishing

Sew the CO edge of the edging to the BO edge.
Weave in all ends and completely soak. This shawl must be blocked quite aggressively; pin the center first, then pin the main body of the shawl out into a circle, and finally pin the edging out into regular points. Leave to dry completely.

Chart A

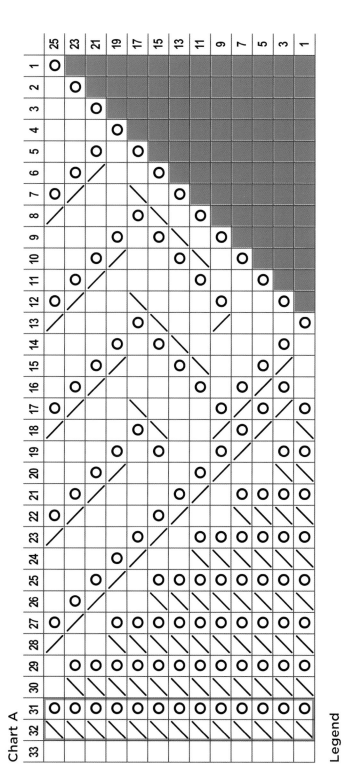

Legend

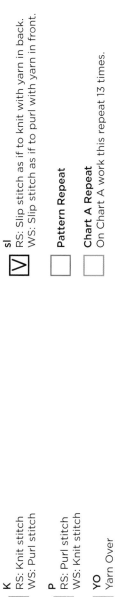

K
RS: Knit stitch
WS: Purl stitch

P
RS: Purl stitch
WS: Knit stitch

YO
Yarn Over

K with Next TBL
Knit stitch together with next shawl body stitch through the back loop.

K2tog
Knit 2 stitches together as 1 stitch.

SSK
Slip 1 stitch as if to knit. Slip another stitch as if to knit. Insert LH needle into front of these 2 stitches and knit them together.

sl
RS: Slip stitch as if to knit with yarn in back.
WS: Slip stitch as if to purl with yarn in front.

Pattern Repeat

Chart A Repeat
On Chart A work this repeat 13 times.

Chart B Repeat
On Chart B work this repeat 4 times.

Chart C Repeat
On Chart C work this repeat 11 times.

No Stitch

Chart B

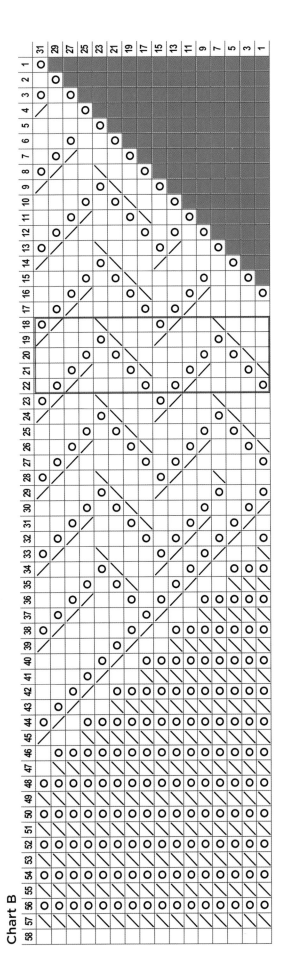

Chart C

Column numbers (left to right): 25 23 21 19 17 15 13 11 9 7 5 3 1

Row numbers (top to bottom): 1 2 3 4 5 6 7 8 9 10 11 12 13 14 15 16 17 18 19 20 21 22 23 24 25 26 27 28 29 30 31 32 33 34 35

Edging Chart

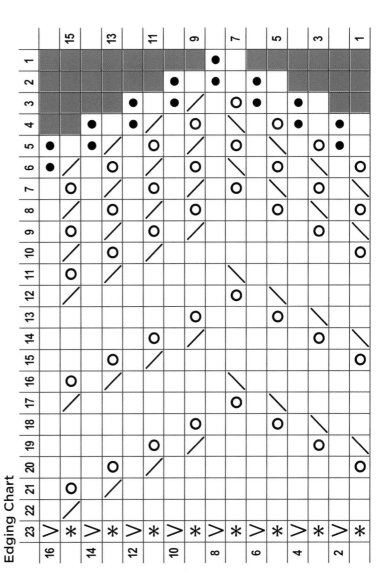

Chart D

DIAMAS

by Susanna IC

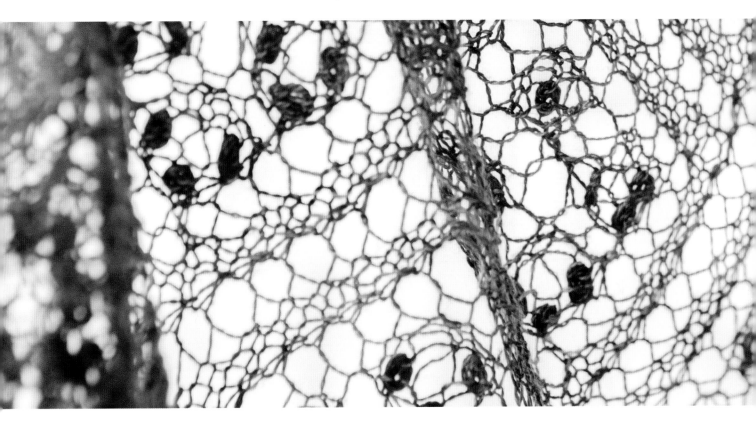

FINISHED MEASUREMENTS

32" back depth, 63" long wingspan

YARN

Knit Picks Luminance Hand Painted
(100% Silk; 439 yards/50g): Patience
27437, 2 skeins.

NEEDLES

US 4 (3.5mm) circular needles, or two
sizes smaller than size to obtain gauge.

US 6 (4mm) circular needles, or size to
obtain gauge in Garter stitch.

US 7 (4.5mm) circular needles, or one
size larger than size to obtain gauge.

US 8 (5mm) circular needles, or two
sizes larger than size to obtain gauge.

US 9 (5.5mm) needle, or three sizes
larger than size to obtain gauge, for bind
off only.

NOTIONS

Yarn Needle
Stitch Markers
Blocking Pins

GAUGE

24 sts and 36 rows = 4" in Garter stitch,
unblocked.

Correct gauge is not critical for this
project, but your final measurements
and yardage requirements will vary if
your gauge is different.

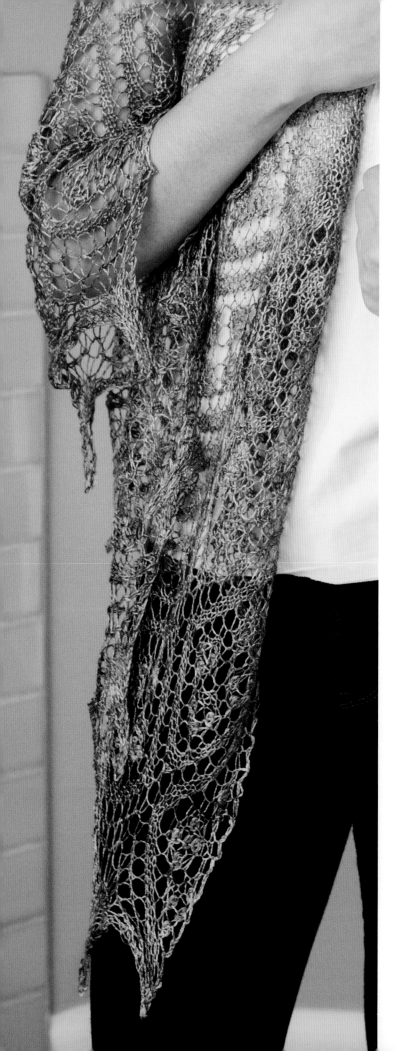

Notes:

I love nupps which adorn the traditional Estonian lace. The idea that these little bits of texture cannot be duplicated by any machine really appeals to me; this makes the gossamer hand-knits even more special. Diamas is a generously-sized crescent worked from the top down, beginning with simple garter stitch short rows, which flow seamlessly into the garter diamonds and lace motifs. At the bottom, the lace border ends with elongated openwork points, which are created with rapid increases. The lace is worked with nupps throughout, but those are optional and can be left off or replaced with beads.

A firm cast on is critical to the success of this project because the crescent shape needs to be supported during blocking to allow the lace points to stretch.

The Bind off needs to be loose to allow for the lace points to block fully; go up in needle size if your bind off feels too tight.

The charts are read from right to left on RS rows (odd numbers), and left to right on WS rows (even numbers).

Short Rows (W&T): Bring yarn to front of work between needles; Sl next st to RH needle; bring yarn around this st to back of work and Sl the st back to LH needle; turn work to begin working in the other direction. The Short Rows wraps can be left unworked, hidden within the garter texture.

No Stitch: This is just a place holder in the chart, there is no actual st on the needles corresponding to this square due to extra decreases. Simply ignore this and work the following square as charted.

Nupp: On the RS loosely work (K, YO, K, YO, K, YO, K) into one st, on the next WS row P all 7 sts tog; one st remains

DIRECTIONS

Top Edge
With US 4 (3.5mm) needles firmly CO 170 sts.
K 1 row TBL (twist sts).
Switch to US 6 (4mm) needles and K 1 row TBL.

Short Rows
Row 1 (RS): K5, PM, K to last 5 sts, W&T.
Row 2 (WS): K5, PM, K to next M, remove M, W&T.
Row 3 (RS): K5, PM, K to next M, remove M, W&T.
Rep Rows 2-3 until fewer than 10 sts are left unworked on the right side at the center, ending with a WS row.

While working the next two rows, please remove all stitch markers.
Next Row (RS): K to end of row leaving wraps in place, turn. Confirm that the number of sts on the needles remains the same (170 sts); if different, make any necessary adjustments (increase or decrease) at the edges of the following row.
Next Row (WS): K to end leaving wraps in place, turn.
K 2 rows.

Lace

Work Rows 1 – 25 of Chart A (13 pattern reps plus edges; you may want to place a stitch marker after each pattern rep). Switch to US 7 (4.5mm) needles and work Rows 26 – 38 of Chart A, then Rows 1 – 39 of Chart B. Switch to US 8 (5mm) needles and work Rows 40 – 55 of Chart B. Then work Chart C, ending after Row 5.

Bind Off

With largest needle BO next WS row as follows: *K2tog, K1, return sts to LH needle, rep from * to end.

Finishing

Weave in all loose ends. Block piece to measurements and shape as shown in the blocking schematic. Start with the two short sides followed by the lace center point, then pin out the rest of the points along the bottom edge (no pins are required along the top CO edge). When completely dry, remove pins and trim all yarn tails.

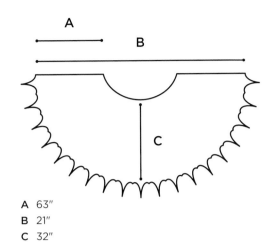

A 63"
B 21"
C 32"

Chart A

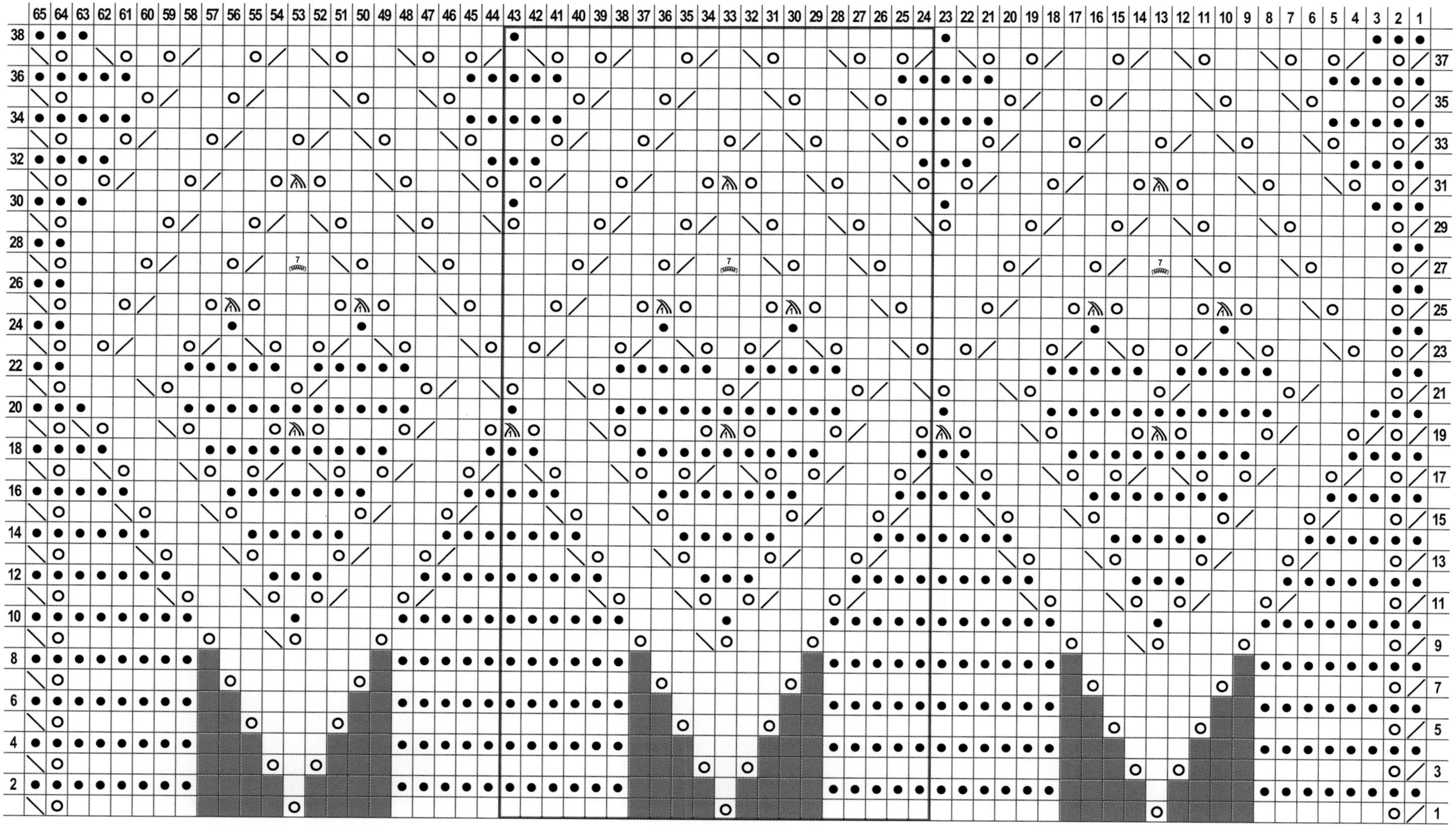

Note: The legend for this chart is located on the following page.

Legend

K
RS: Knit stitch
WS: Purl stitch

P
RS: Purl stitch
WS: Knit stitch

YO
Yarn Over

K2tog
Knit 2 stitches together as 1 stitch.

SSK
Slip 1 stitch as if to knit. Slip another stitch as if to knit.
Insert LH needle into front of these 2 stitches and knit
them together.

sl2 K1 PSSO
Slip 2 stitches. Knit 1 then pass the slipped stitches over.

KYOK
K1 and leave on needle. YO, then knit again into the
same st to make 3 sts from 1.

7-Stitch Nupp
On the RS loosely work (K, YO, K, YO, K, YO, K) into 1
stitch. On the next WS row purl all 7 stitches together.
1 stitch remains.

No Stitch

Pattern Repeat

Chart B

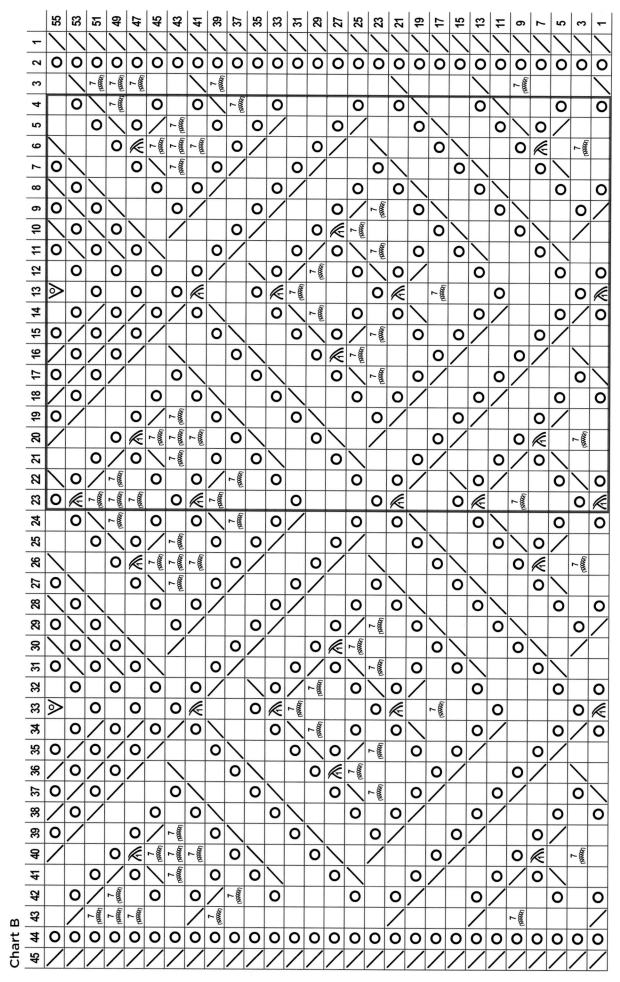

Note: Work all WS rows as K2, P to last 2 stitches, K2. Close all nupps with P7tog.

Chart C

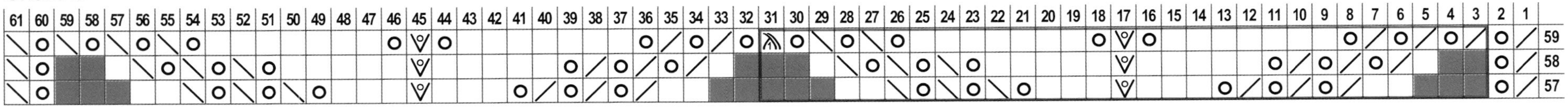

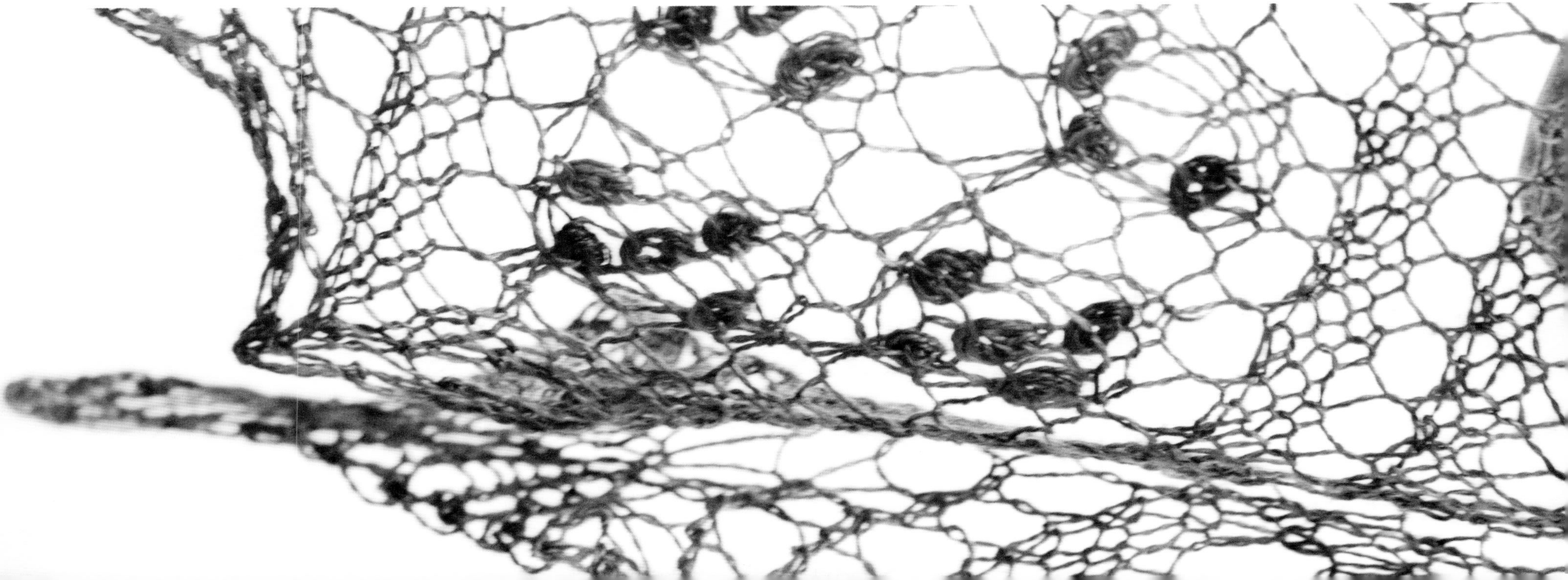

DIAMONDS AND ROSES CARDIGAN

by Heather Pfeifer

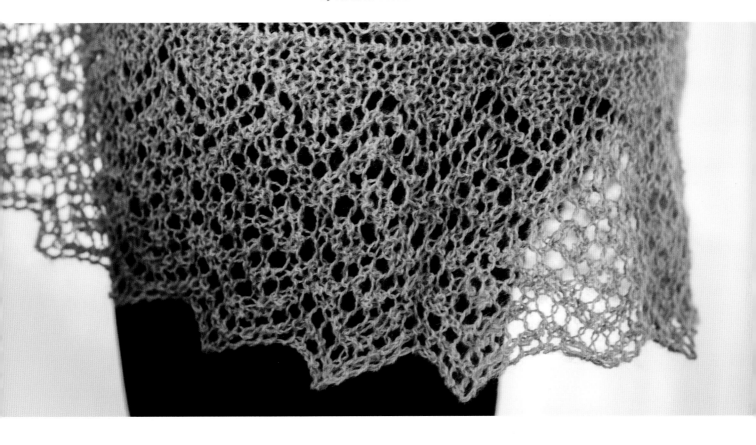

FINISHED MEASUREMENTS

36" (37.5, 40.5, 42, 45, 46.25, 48, 49.25, 52.25, 54, 55)" finished bust measurement

Garment is meant to be worn with 2-4" of positive ease at chest

YARN

Knit Picks Alpaca Cloud Lace Yarn (100% Baby Alpaca; 440 yards/50g): Augusta 26796, 3 (3, 3, 3, 3, 3, 4, 4, 4, 4, 4) skeins.

NEEDLES

US 4 (3.5mm) 16" and 24-32" circular needles, or size to obtain gauge

US 8 (5mm) DPN for 3-Needle Bind Off

NOTIONS

Yarn Needle
4 Stitch Markers
1 Split Ring Marker
Scrap Yarn
Blocking Wires and Pins

GAUGE

22 sts and 48 rows = 4.25" x 3-7/16" in Garter stitch, unblocked.

22 sts and 48 rows = 4" in Garter stitch, blocked.

23 sts and 36 rows = 4" over Mesh Lace pattern, blocked.

41 sts and 36 rows = 8" x 4" over sts 17-57 of Body Chart, blocked.

For pattern support, contact
amethystknits@shaw.ca

Notes:

A classic A-line silhouette with lace soft enough for the boudoir, this garter-based open cardigan showcases a girl's best friends: diamonds and roses. Beginning with the lower hem, stitches are then picked up and the body is worked up to the underarms, where fronts and back are split. Shoulders are joined and stitches picked up to work short-row sleeve caps. The sleeves are finished with the same lace edging as the lower hem, worked as a knitted on edging and binding off all sleeve sts. Finally, stitches are picked up for the garter-stitch front bands and back neck, then finished with an I-Cord bind off.

This is a garter-stitch based pattern with lace worked on RS and WS.

Recommendations for this pattern are to use knitting needles with sharp tips, use lightweight stitch markers, mark RS of work, and use lifelines according to preference. The K2tog TBL and SSK are interchangeable according to preference, the K3tog must always be worked TBL.

Charts are read from right to left on RS rows (odd numbers) and left to right on WS rows (even numbers).

Please note that the K and K3tog TBL stitches are represented by the same symbol on both the RS and WS.

Mesh Lace (worked flat over multiples of 4 sts plus 3)
Row 1 (RS): Knit.
Row 2 (WS): K1, YO, (K3togTBL, YO, K1, YO) to last 2 sts, SSK.
Row 3: Knit.
Row 4: K2tog, YO, (K1, YO, K3togTBL, YO) to last st, K1.
Rep Rows 1-4 for pattern.

Jeny's Surprisingly Stretchy Bind Off
Step 1: YO right needle in reverse.
Step 2: K1.
Step 3: Pass YO over K st and off needle.
Steps 4-5: Rep Step 1-2.
Step 6: Pass YO and first K st tog as one off needle.
Rep Steps 4-6 until desired number of sts have been bound off.

3-Needle Bind-off
Hold the two pieces of knitting with right sides together and the needle tips facing to the right. Insert a third needle (DPN) into the first st on each of the needles K-wise, starting with the front needle. Knit the st on the front needle together with the st on the back needle. Repeat this motion, inserting your needle into one st on the front and back needles, knitting them together and slipping them off the needles. Each time you complete a second st, pass the first finished st over the second and off of the needle (as you would in a traditional BO). When one st remains on right needle, break yarn and draw tail out of the st to secure. Weave in end.

Cable Cast On
*Insert right needle between first and second sts on the left needle. Wrap yarn as if to knit, draw loop between sts. Insert left needle into loop from bottom up. Rep from *.

DIRECTIONS

Hem
CO 13 sts using Long Tail method.
Setup Row (WS): Knit.
Work Rows 1-18 of Hem Chart once.
Work Rows 19-36 of Hem Chart 20 (21, 23, 24, 25, 26, 27, 28, 30, 31, 32) times total.
Work Rows 37-53 of Hem Chart once.
BO very loosely K-wise on WS. Draw ball of yarn through remaining st. Tighten knot but do not break yarn.

Body
Lay hem with YO edge at top, and working yarn still attached to the right top corner.
PU the loops beginning at the left edge, from front to back using longer circular needle. 198 (207, 225, 234, 243, 252, 261, 270, 288, 297, 306) sts.

Setup Row (WS): Knit all sts TBL, evenly increasing (+) by YO, or decreasing (-) by K2tog as follows: +3 (+2, 0, -1, +6, +5, +4, +3, +1, 0, -1). 201 (209, 225, 233, 249, 257, 265, 273, 289, 297, 305) sts.

The first 2 rows below correspond to Rows 1-2 of Body Chart and set the markers (blue vertical lines on Body Chart), and establishes Mesh Lace pattern.
Row 1 (RS): K2, K2tog, YO, K1, YO, SSK, K2, PM, K71 (75, 83, 87, 95, 99, 103, 107, 115, 119, 123), PM, K2, K2tog, YO, K1, YO, SSK, K10, YO, K3togTBL, YO, K1, YO, K3togTBL, YO, K10, K2tog, YO, K1, YO, SSK, K2, PM, K71 (75, 83, 87, 95, 99, 103, 107, 115, 119, 123), PM, K2, K2tog, YO, K1, YO, SSK, K2.
Row 2 (WS): K9, SM, K1, YO (K3togTBL, YO, K1, YO) to 2 sts before M, SSK, SM, K to M, SM, K1, (YO, K3togTBL, YO, K1) to 2 sts before M, YO, SSK, SM, K9.
Rows 3-108: Continue Body Chart as established, repeating the chart a total of three times.

Rows 109-121: Corresponds to Rows 1-13 of the 4th repeat of Body Chart. Use Decrease Chart Right in place of Body Chart sts 10-16, and Decrease Chart Left in place of Body Chart sts 58-64. 193 (201, 217, 225, 241, 249, 257, 265, 281, 289, 297) sts.
Row 122: Return to Body Chart Row 14.

Begin Underarm Bind Off on Row 7 (3, 1, 35, 31, 29, 27, 25, 25, 23, 21) of the 5 (5, 5, 4, 4, 4, 4, 4, 4, 4, 4)th rep of the Body Chart as follows:
Work 42 (44, 46, 46, 50, 52, 52, 54, 56, 56, 57) sts as established according to the Body Chart, using Jeny's Surprisingly Stretchy Bind Off, BO 12 (12, 16, 20, 20, 20, 24, 24, 28, 32, 34) sts, work the next 84 (89, 93, 93, 101, 105, 105, 109, 113, 113, 115) sts according to the Body Chart, BO 12 (12, 16, 20, 20, 20, 24, 24, 28, 32, 34) sts using Jeny's Surprisingly Stretchy Bind Off, work as established according to chart to end. Total sts (front/back/front): 42/85/42 (44/89/44, 46/93/46, 46/93/46, 50/101/50, 52/105/52, 52/105/52, 54/109/54, 56/113/56, 56/113/56, 57/115/57).

Notes:
Armscye edges must have a selvedge of 1 st in St st and 1 st in Garter next to it.
If (YO, K3togTBL, YO) cannot be completed, substitute with (YO, SSK), and if that cannot be completed, then knit remaining sts.

Left Front
Next Row (WS): Work as established in Body Chart to last st, P1.
Dec Row (RS): K1, K2tog, work remaining sts as established. 1 st dec.
Rep previous two rows 5 (7, 9, 9, 9, 11, 11, 13, 15, 15, 12) more times. 36 (36, 36, 36, 40, 40, 40, 40, 40, 40, 44) Left Front sts.
Maintaining selvedge on armscye edge only, work even, completing Row 20 of the 5th rep of Body Chart.

Left Neck Shaping
Beginning on Row 21 of 5th repeat of Body Chart, begin neck shaping, maintaining the Mesh Pattern shown on Body Chart sts 58-73. Work decreases as follows:
Dec Row (RS): K to 2 sts before last M, SSK, SM, work as established to end. 1 st dec.
Next Row (WS): Work even as established to last st, P1.
Rep previous two rows 17 (18, 19, 19, 20, 21, 21, 21, 21, 22, 22) more times. 18 (17, 16, 16, 19, 18, 18, 18, 18, 17, 21) sts.
Work even, maintaining selvedge on armscye edge for the remainder of the 6th repeat of the Body Chart.
Next Row (RS): Knit.
Place the 18 (17, 16, 16, 19, 18, 18, 18, 18, 17, 21) sts onto scrap yarn for left shoulder seam.

Back

Reattach yarn to WS of Back sts.

Next Row (WS): P1, work as established to last st, P1.

Dec Row (RS): K1, K2tog, work as established to last 3 sts, SSK, K1. 2 sts dec.

Rep previous two rows 5 (7, 9, 9, 9, 11, 11, 13, 15, 15, 12) more times. 73 (73, 73, 73, 81, 81, 81, 81, 81, 81, 89) Back sts.

Complete Row 35 of the 6th rep of Body Chart.

Next Row (WS): P1, K to last st SM as needed, P1.

Place first and last 18 (17, 16, 16, 19, 18, 18, 18, 18, 17, 21) sts onto scrap yarn for shoulders.

Place remaining center 37 (39, 41, 41, 43, 45, 45, 45, 45, 47, 47) sts onto scrap yarn for neck.

Right Front

Reattach yarn to WS of Right Front.

Next Row (WS): P1, work as established to end.

Dec Row (RS): Work as established to the last 3 sts, SSK, K1. 1 st dec.

Rep previous 2 rows 5 (7, 9, 9, 9, 11, 11, 13, 15, 15, 12) more times. 36 (36, 36, 36, 40, 40, 40, 40, 40, 40, 44) Right Front sts.

Maintaining selvedge on armscye edge only, work even, completing Row 20 of the 5th rep of Body Chart.

Right Neck Shaping

Beginning on Row 21 of 5th repeat of Body Chart, begin neck shaping, maintaining the Mesh Pattern shown on Body Chart sts 10-16. Work decreases as follows:

Dec Row (RS): Work as established to first M, SM, K2tog, K to end. 1 st dec.

Next Row (WS): P1, work as established to end.

Rep previous two rows 17 (18, 19, 19, 20, 21, 21, 21, 21, 22, 22) more times. 18 (17, 16, 16, 19, 18, 18, 18, 18, 17, 21) sts.

Work even, maintaining selvedge on armscye edge for the remainder of the 6th repeat of the Body Chart.

Next Row (RS): Knit.

Break yarn, leaving a 12" tail. Place the 18 (17, 16, 16, 19, 18, 18, 18, 18, 17, 21) sts onto scrap yarn for right shoulder seam.

Joining Shoulders

Turn front pieces with RS facing the RS of the back.

Return held shoulders sts of corresponding front and back to needles. Using the larger needle size DPN, join with Three-Needle Bind-off. Rep for second shoulder.

Neck sts remain on scrap yarn. Turn pieces RS out.

Sleeve (Make 2)

Sleeves are worked flat using short rows beginning at top shoulder seam. Each row works 1 st past previous row's worked sts.

With RS facing, begin at center of underarm BO and with shorter circular PU 63 (63, 63, 72, 72, 81, 90, 90, 99, 99, 99) sts.

Place beginning of row M as follows: If st count is even, place M between first and last picked up sts at the underarm, then join as if to work in the rnd. If st count is odd, place split ring M onto (not between) first st of rnd at the underarm, then join as if to work in the rnd.

Row 1 (RS): K31 (31, 31, 36, 36, 40, 45, 45, 49, 49, 49), PM, K4. Turn.

NOTE: M is placed at top of armscye, at the shoulder seam.

Row 2 (WS): K1, YO, K3togTBL, YO, SM, K1, YO, K3togTBL, YO, K1. Turn.

Row 3: K5, SM, K5. Turn.

Row 4: K1, K2tog, YO, K1, YO, SL1, remove M, replace SL st, PM, K3togTBL, YO, K1, YO, SSK, K1. Turn.

Row 5: K6, SM, K6. Turn.

Row 6: K3, YO, K3togTBL, YO, SM, K1, YO, K3togTBL, YO, K3. Turn.

Row 7: K7, SM, K7. Turn.

Row 8: K2, YO, K3togTBL, YO, K1, YO, SL1, remove M, replace SL st, PM, K3togTBL, YO, K1, YO, K3togTBL, YO, K2. Turn.

These 8 rows represent the Sleeve Cap Chart and set up the patterning for the remainder of the sleeve cap.

Each row of the Sleeve Cap Chart works 1 more picked up st of the armscye. On RS rows, the number of sts K to the M will be the number of sts K after the marker.

Continue working Rows 1-8 of the Sleeve Cap Chart, repeating sts in red box twice more on each rep of the Chart until all sts have been worked, excluding the marked st if your armscye had an odd number of sts picked up.

Do not break yarn. 63 (63, 63, 72, 72, 81, 90, 90, 99, 99, 99) sts.

Using the Cable Cast On method, CO 21 sts onto LH needle, next to Sleeve Cap sts.

Begin Row 1 of Sleeve Edge Chart. Note that the last st of the Sleeve Edge Chart is a decrease, which joins the lace edging to the Sleeve Cap sts.

At the end of each RS Sleeve Edge Chart row, turn work, K to end.

Rep Sleeve Edge Chart 6 (6, 6, 7, 7, 8, 9, 9, 10, 10, 10) times.

Work Rows 1-17 of Sleeve Edge Chart once more.

Row 18: BO loosely K-wise.

Seam CO and BO edges together.

Rep all for second sleeve cap.

Edge Band and Neck Finishing

With longer circular, RS facing and beginning at the bottom of the right front hem, PU 1 st every other row to held neck sts, replace sts from scrap yarn onto needle, K across back neck, continue picking up sts to the bottom of the front left hem. Exact st count unnecessary.

Row 1 (WS): P1, K to last st, P1.

Row 2 (RS): K1, SSK, K to last 3 sts, K2tog, K1. 2 sts dec.

Row 3: Rep Row 1.

Work an I-cord BO on RS as follows:
Cable CO 3 sts. *K2, K2togTBL, replace 3 sts to left needle. Rep from * to last st on left needle.

K4tog TBL, break yarn and draw tail through.

Finishing

Weave in ends, wash and block to diagram using lace wires as follows:

Overlap front edge bands. Weave lace wire through both from hem to beginning of neck shaping. Pin shoulder width to diagram. Insert lace wires from underarm to hem on each side. Pin at desired chest width. Spread hem outwards to diagram width or desired hip width. Pin each point of lace hem. Insert lace wires along top and underarm edges of sleeve caps to diagram or desired width. Pin each point of sleeve hem. Open neck lace edging and pin as desired.

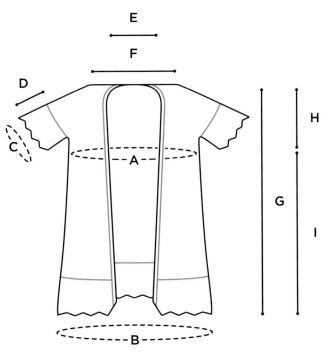

A 36 (37.5, 40.5, 42, 45, 46.25, 48, 49.25, 52.25, 54, 55)"
B 37 (38, 42, 43, 45, 47, 48, 50, 53, 55, 57)"
C 11.5 (11.5, 11.5, 13.25, 13.25, 15, 16.5, 16.5, 18.25, 18.25, 18.25)"
D 5", all sizes
E 7 (7.5, 8, 8, 8.25, 8.75, 8.75, 8.75, 8.75, 9, 9)"
F 14 (14, 14, 14, 15.5, 15.5, 15.5, 15.5, 15.5, 15.5, 16.75)"
G 29", all sizes
H 7 (7.5, 7.75, 8, 8.5, 8.75, 9, 9, 9, 9.25, 9.5)"
I 22 (21.5, 21, 21, 20.5, 20.25, 20, 20, 20, 19.75, 19.5)"

Legend

K
RS: Knit stitch
WS: Knit stitch

YO
Yarn Over

K2tog
RS: Knit 2 stitches together as 1 stitch.
WS: (SSK) Slip 1 stitch as if to knit. Slip another stitch as if to knit. Insert LH needle into front of these 2 stitches and knit them together.

SSK
RS: Slip 1 stitch as if to knit. Slip another stitch as if to knit. Insert LH needle into front of these 2 stitches and knit them together.
WS: (K2tog) Knit 2 stitches together as 1 stitch.

K3tog TBL
Knit 3 stitches together through back loops.

Turn No Stitch
Turn your work. No stitch.

No Stitch

Pattern Repeat

Place Marker

Hem Chart

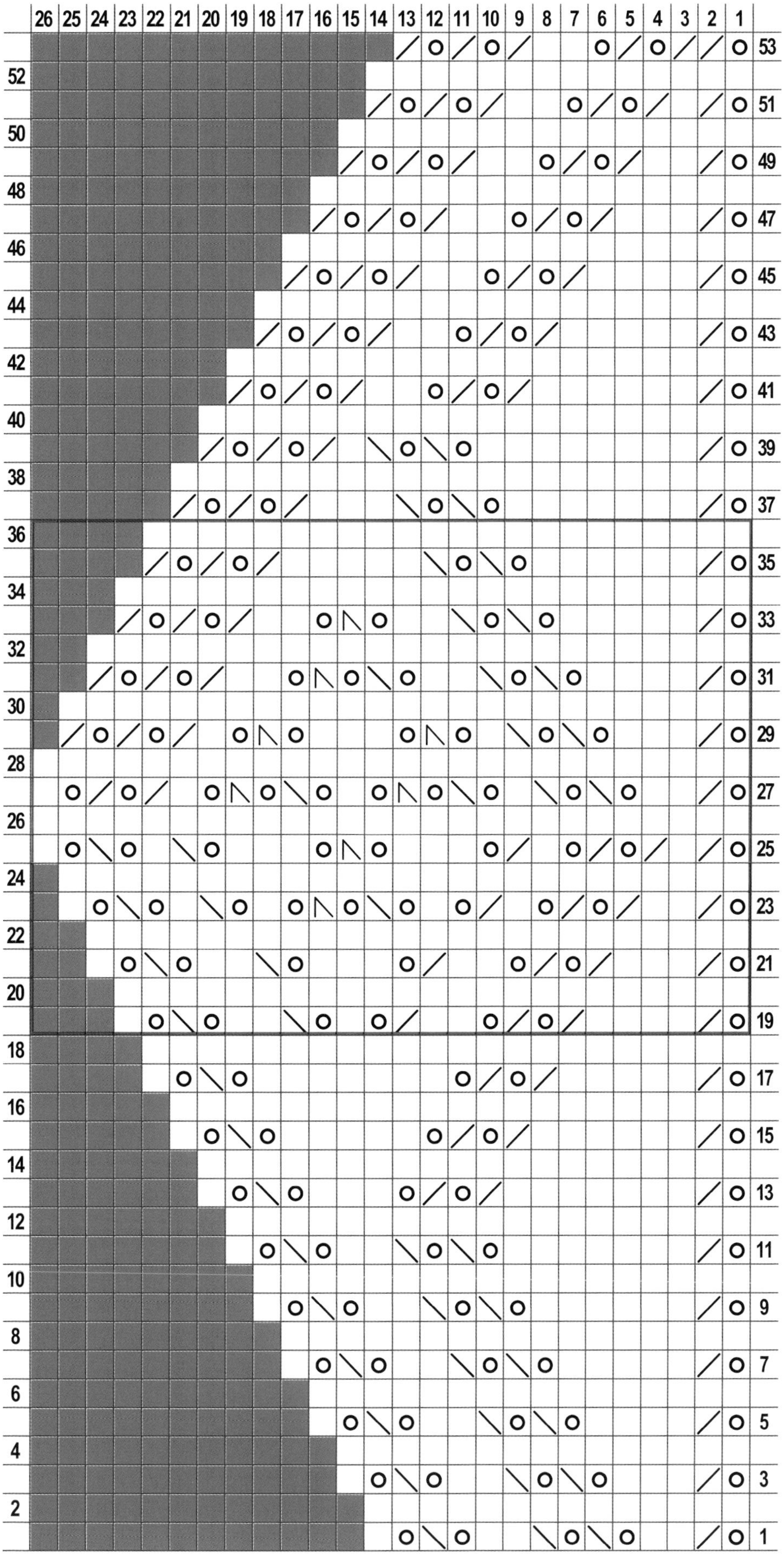

Body Chart

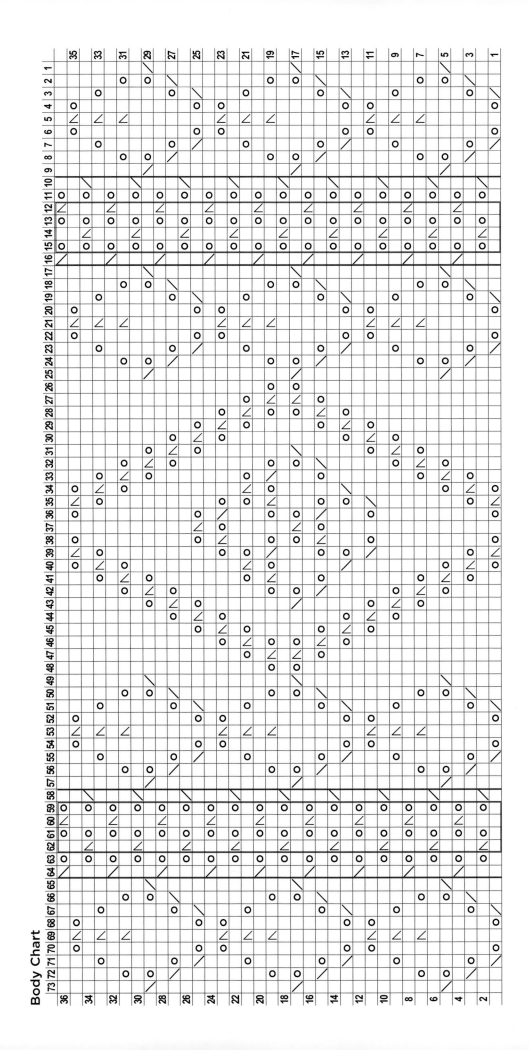

Decrease Right Chart

	11	10	9	8	7	6	5	4	3	2	1	
	■	■	■	■	\							13
12	■	■	■		\	O		O	Λ	O		
	■	■	■									11
10	■	■	■			O	Λ	O		O	/	
	■	■		\								9
8	■	■		O	\	O		O	Λ	O		
	■	■										7
6	■					O	Λ	O		O	/	
	■		\									5
4	■			O	\	O		O	Λ	O		
	■											3
2	■		\		O	O	Λ	O		O	/	
	■	\										1

Decrease Left Chart

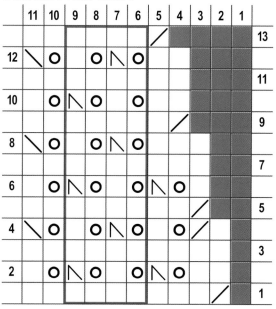

Sleeve Cap Chart

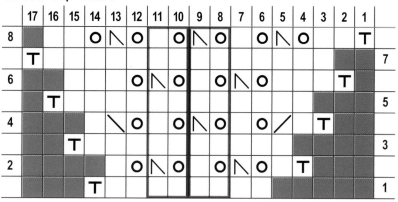

Sleeve Hem Chart

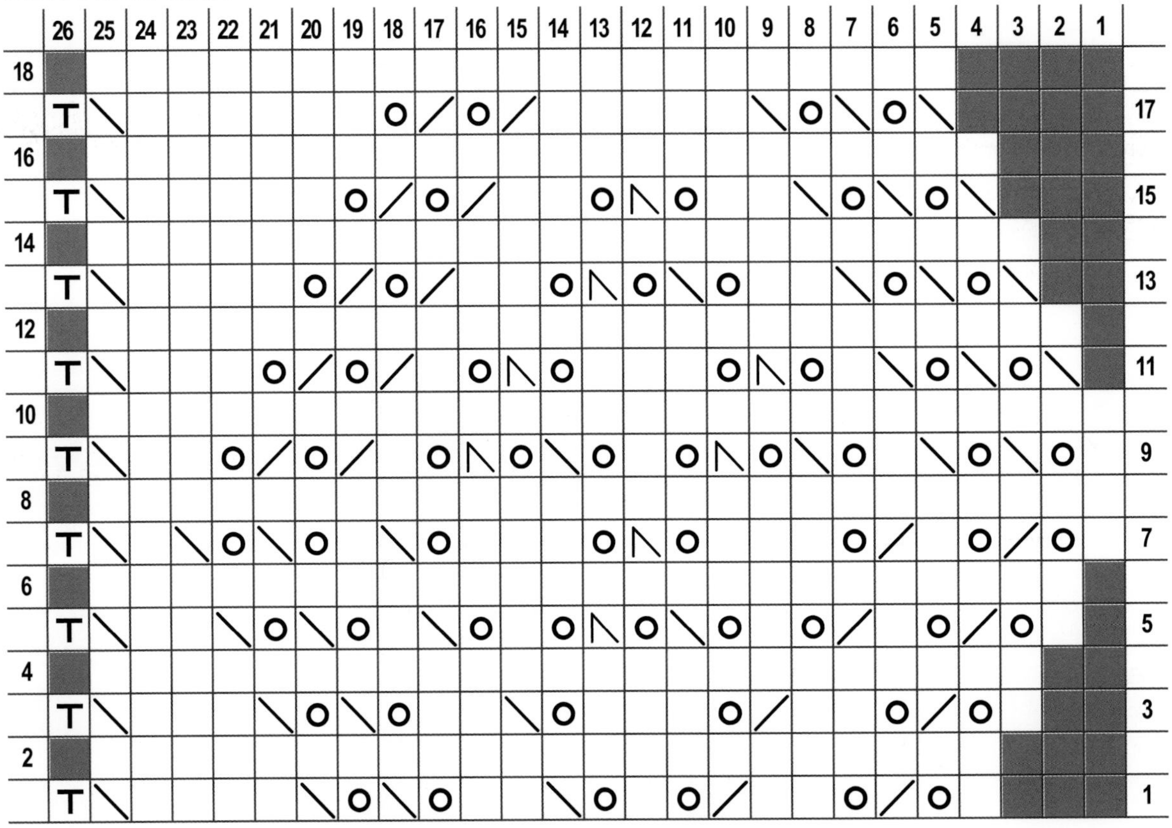

	26	25	24	23	22	21	20	19	18	17	16	15	14	13	12	11	10	9	8	7	6	5	4	3	2	1	
18	▨																						▨	▨	▨	▨	
	T	\							O	/	O	/						\	O	\	O	\	▨	▨	▨	▨	17
16	▨																							▨	▨	▨	
	T	\					O	/	O	/		O	∧	O		\	O	\	O	\				▨	▨	▨	15
14	▨																								▨	▨	
	T	\				O	/	O	/		O	∧	O	\	O		\	O	\	O	\				▨	▨	13
12	▨																									▨	
	T	\			O	/	O	/		O	∧	O			O	∧	O			\	O	\	O	\		▨	11
10	▨																										
	T	\		O	/	O	/		O	∧	O	\	O		O	∧	O	\	O		\	O	\	O			9
8	▨																									▨	
	T	\		\	O	\	O		\	O			O	∧	O			O	/		O	/	O			▨	7
6	▨																								▨	▨	
	T	\			\	O	\	O		\	O		O	∧	O	\	O		O	/		O	/	O	▨	▨	5
4	▨																							▨	▨	▨	
	T	\				\	O	\	O			\	O			O	/			O	/	O		▨	▨	▨	3
2	▨																						▨	▨	▨	▨	
	T	\					\	O	\	O			\	O		O	/			O	/	O	▨	▨	▨	▨	1

GATHERING FEATHERS SHAWL

by Alina Appasova

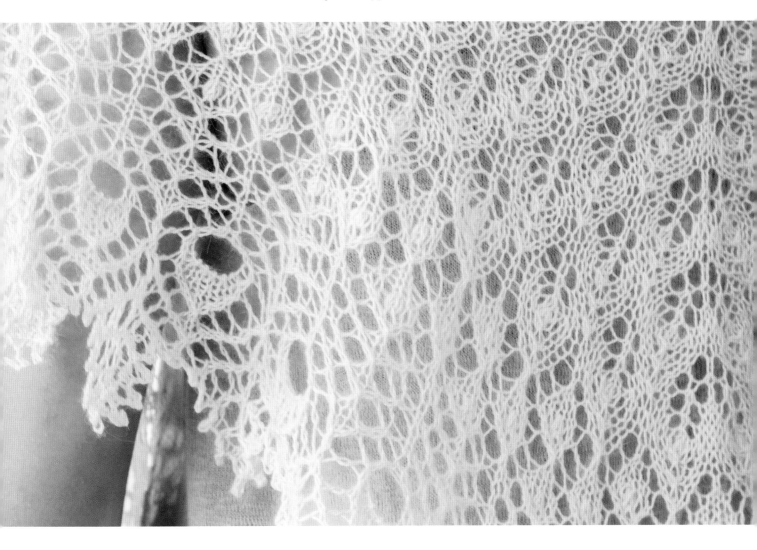

FINISHED MEASUREMENTS

26" deep x 54" wide

YARN

Knit Picks Shimmer
(70% Baby Alpaca, 30% Silk; 880
yards/100g): Bare Shimmer 26584, 1 skein.

NEEDLES

US 3 (3.25mm) 24" or longer circular
needles, or size to obtain gauge

NOTIONS

Yarn Needle
4 Stitch Markers
Blocking Pins

GAUGE

21 sts and 32 rows = 4" over lace
patterns, blocked (Gauge for this project
is approximate but differences will affect
finished size and yarn requirements).

For pattern support, contact
appasov@gmail.com

Notes:

Gathering Feathers is a lace shawl inspired by the beauty and ephemeral nature of peacock feathers. The shawl starts at the neck with pretty, simple patterning, and as you go further the stitches get more interesting and complex. A Picot bind-off adds delicate decorative touches to the shawl edges.

This triangular shawl is constructed flat, with increases at each end and at the center stitch on every odd row to create the triangle shape. It is worked from the center top edge to the bottom edging.

All rows are worked with three edge stitches in Garter stitch. These stitches, as well as the center stitch of Charts 1 and 2, are not included on the charts but are included in the total stitch counts.

To increase the size of the shawl, work additional repeats of Chart 2. Each additional repeat of Chart 2 will result in an increase of 16 stitches per repeat (+40 sts before bind off). After Chart 2 is complete, center stitch markers are removed and shaping increases will continue only along edges. No center stitch.

In Charts 7, 8, and 9, additional increases will be made into each repeat across the row. This will increase the stitch count rapidly. Boxed areas of charts indicate stitch pattern repeat across rows. See instructions below for additional information. Use stitch markers at center stitch and to indicate the 3 edge sts on each side.

Picot BO: *CO 2 sts using Cable Cast On, BO 4 sts, place resulting st on RH needle back on the LH needle; rep from * until all sts are BO. Cut yarn and draw through remaining st.

DIRECTIONS

Garter Tab Cast On

CO 3 sts using the Long Tail CO. Knit 2 rows.

K across, do not turn work. Rotate piece 90 degrees clockwise; PU and K 1 st from garter st ridge along adjacent edge of piece. 4 sts. Rotate piece again, 90 degrees clockwise; PU and K3 sts, 1 st in each CO st, along CO edge. 7 sts.

Work Charts

Set Up Row (WS): K3, P1, K3. 7 sts.

PM's for edges and center st:

Row 1 (RS): K3, PM, YO, PM, K1, PM, YO, PM, K3. 9 sts. This is Row 1 of Chart 1.

Row 2 (WS): K3, P3, K3. 9 sts.

For Charts 1 and 2, odd numbered rows (RS) are worked right to left as: K3, SM, work chart row, SM, K1 center st, SM, rep chart row again, SM, K3. Even numbered rows (WS), not shown on the charts, are worked as: K3, SM, P until the last M, K3.

Chart 1: Work Rows 3-16 once. 37 sts.

Chart 2: Work Rows 1-8 ten times. Boxed stitch pattern is repeated two times for first rep, three times for the second, and so on. 197 sts.

For Charts 3 and 4, odd numbered rows (RS) are worked right to left as: K3, SM, work chart, SM, K3. Even numbered rows (WS) are worked as: K3, SM, P until the last marker and P5tog to close the nupps, SM, K3. Work the nupps loosely on RS rows, to facilitate the P5tog.

As you work the first row of Chart 3 remove both center st Ms.

Chart 3: Work Rows 1-2 once. Boxed stitch pattern is repeated 23 times. 199 sts.

Chart 4: Work Rows 1-14 once. Boxed stitch pattern is repeated 24 times. 221 sts.

For Chart 5, odd numbered rows (RS) are worked right to left as: K3, SM, work chart row, SM, K3 sts. Even numbered rows (WS) are worked from left to right as: K3, SM, P until the last M, K3.

Chart 5: Work Rows 1-10 once. Boxed stitch pattern is repeated 26 times. 231 sts.

For Chart 6, RS AND WS rows are worked right to left as: K3, SM, work chart row, SM, K3 sts.

Chart 6: Work Rows 1-4 once. Boxed stitch pattern is repeated 27 times. 233 sts.

For Charts 7, 8, and 9, odd numbered rows (RS) are worked right to left as: K3, SM, work chart row, SM, K3. Even numbered rows (WS) are worked from left to right as: K3, SM, P until the last M, K3.

Chart 7: Work Rows 1-10 once. Boxed stitch pattern is repeated 28 times. 353 sts.

Chart 8: Work Rows 1-2 once. Boxed stitch pattern is repeated 28 times. 471 sts.

Chart 9: Work Rows 1-2 once. Boxed stitch pattern is repeated 28 times. 589 sts.

Next Row (WS): K2tog once. Put resulting st back on the LH needle.

Bind Off

BO on RS, using the Picot BO.

Finishing

Weave in ends, wash, and block to size.

Legend

Symbol	Name	Description
□	**K**	Knit stitch
O	**YO**	Yarn Over
╱	**K2tog**	Knit 2 stitches together as 1 stitch.
╲	**SSK**	Slip 1 stitch as if to knit. Slip another stitch as if to knit. Insert LH needle into front of these 2 stitches and knit them together.
人	**sl1 K2tog PSSO (SK2P)**	Slip 1 stitch. K2tog then pass the slipped stitch over.
◣	**Right Leaning Increase**	Lift the stitch below the stitch on the LH needle and knit it. Then knit the stitch from the current row.
5	**Nupp**	On the RS loosely work (K, YO, K, YO, K) into 1 stitch. On the next WS row purl all 5 stitches together. 1 stitch remains.
◹	**KYOK**	K1 and leave on needle. YO, then knit again into the same st to make 3 sts from 1.
5	**M5**	(K1, YO, K1, YO, K1) into 1 stitch.
7	**M7**	(K1, YO, K1, YO, K1, YO, K1) into 1 stitch.
⊥	**Star Stitch**	K3tog, leaving stitch on LH needle. (K1, YO, K1) into 1 stitch, then drop all stitches from LH needle.
▓	**No Stitch**	
□	**Pattern Repeat**	

Chart 1

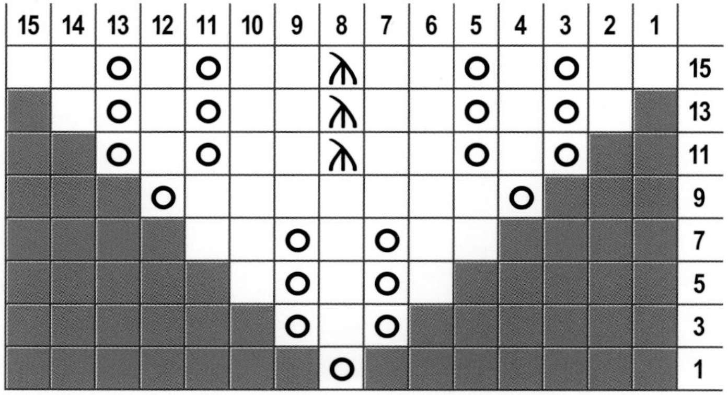

Columns (top): 15 14 13 12 11 10 9 8 7 6 5 4 3 2 1
Rows (right): 15 13 11 9 7 5 3 1

Chart 2

Columns (top): 23 22 21 20 19 18 17 16 15 14 13 12 11 10 9 8 7 6 5 4 3 2 1
Rows (right): 7 5 3 1

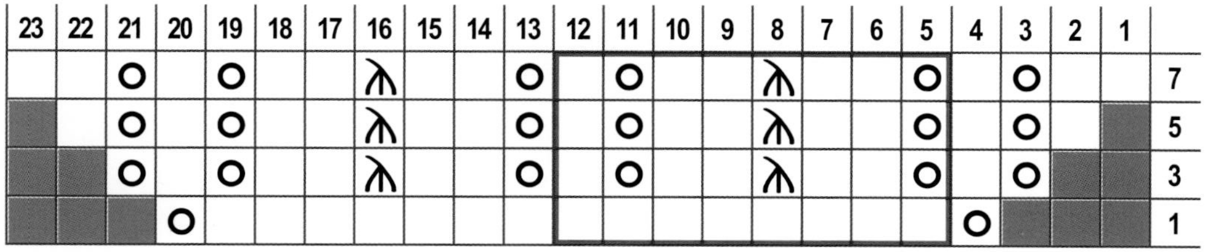

Chart 3

Columns (top): 17 16 15 14 13 12 11 10 9 8 7 6 5 4 3 2 1
Rows (right): 1

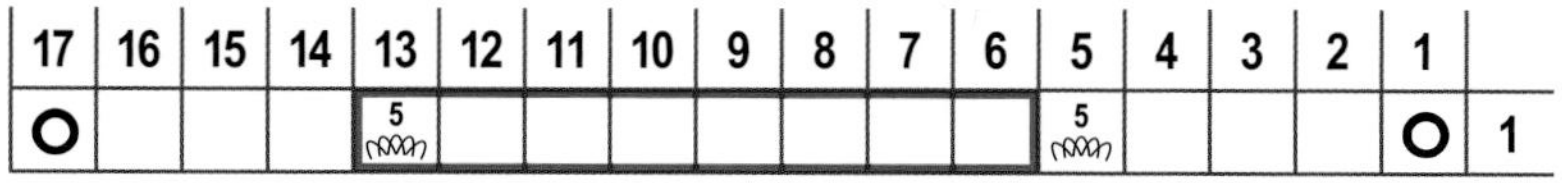

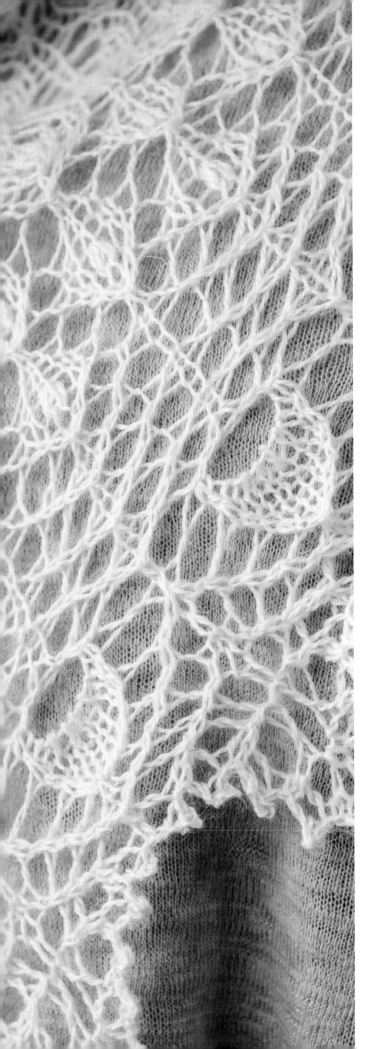

Chart 4

Chart 5

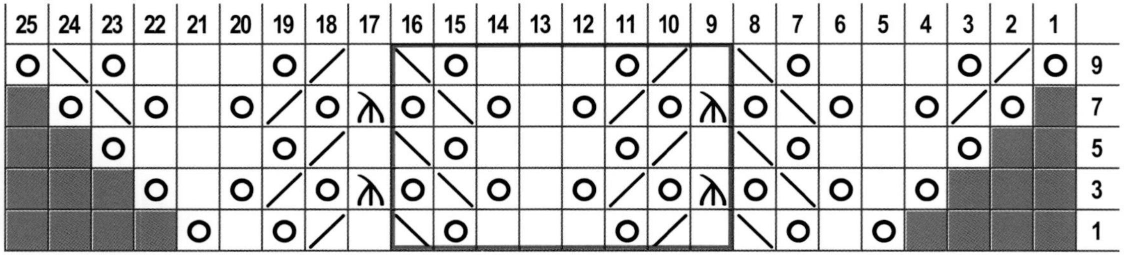

Columns: 9, 7, 5, 3, 1
Rows: 1, 2, 3, 4, 5, 6, 7, 8, 9, 10, 11, 12, 13, 14, 15, 16, 17, 18, 19, 20, 21, 22, 23, 24, 25

Chart 6

Columns: 4, 3, 2, 1
Rows: 1, 2, 3, 4, 5, 6, 7, 8, 9, 10, 11, 12, 13, 14, 15, 16, 17, 18, 19

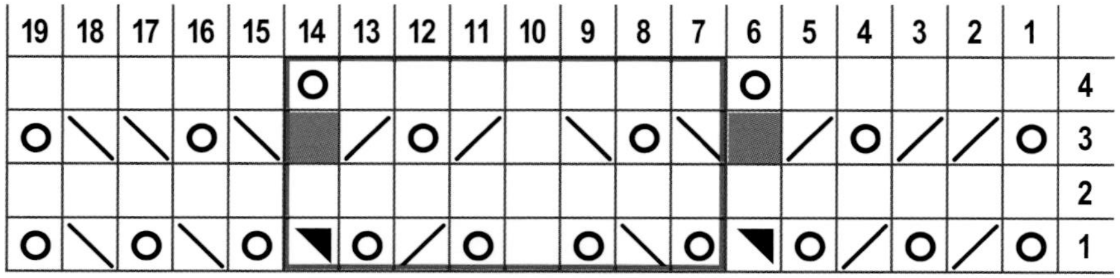

Chart 7

Columns: 9, 7, 5, 3, 1
Rows: 1, 2, 3, 4, 5, 6, 7, 8, 9, 10, 11, 12, 13, 14, 15, 16, 17, 18, 19, 20, 21, 22, 23

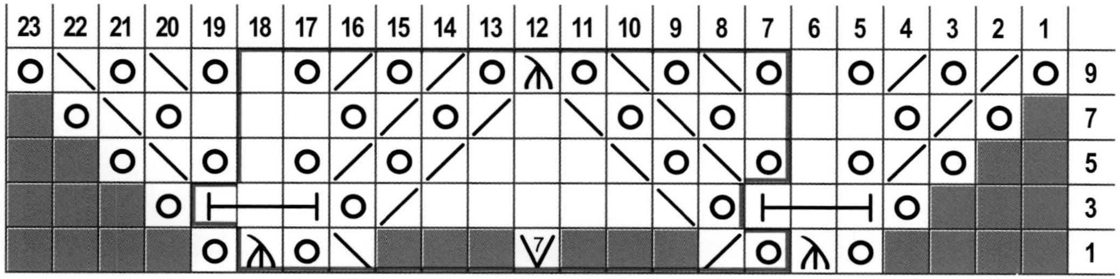

A

A 54"
B 26"

Chart 8

25	24	23	22	21	20	19	18	17	16	15	14	13	12	11	10	9	8	7	6	5	4	3	2	1
O		/	O		⍑		O	/	O	/	O	/	/	O	/	O		⍑	O	/	/	O	/	O

Chart 9

43	42	41	40	39	38	37	36	35	34	33	32	31	30	29	28	27	26	25	24	23	22	21	20	19	18	17	16	15	14	13	12	11	10	9	8	7	6	5	4	3	2	1
O		/	O		/		O		O		O		O		O		O	O	/	O	/	⍓	O	O	/		O		O		O		O		O		/		O		/	O

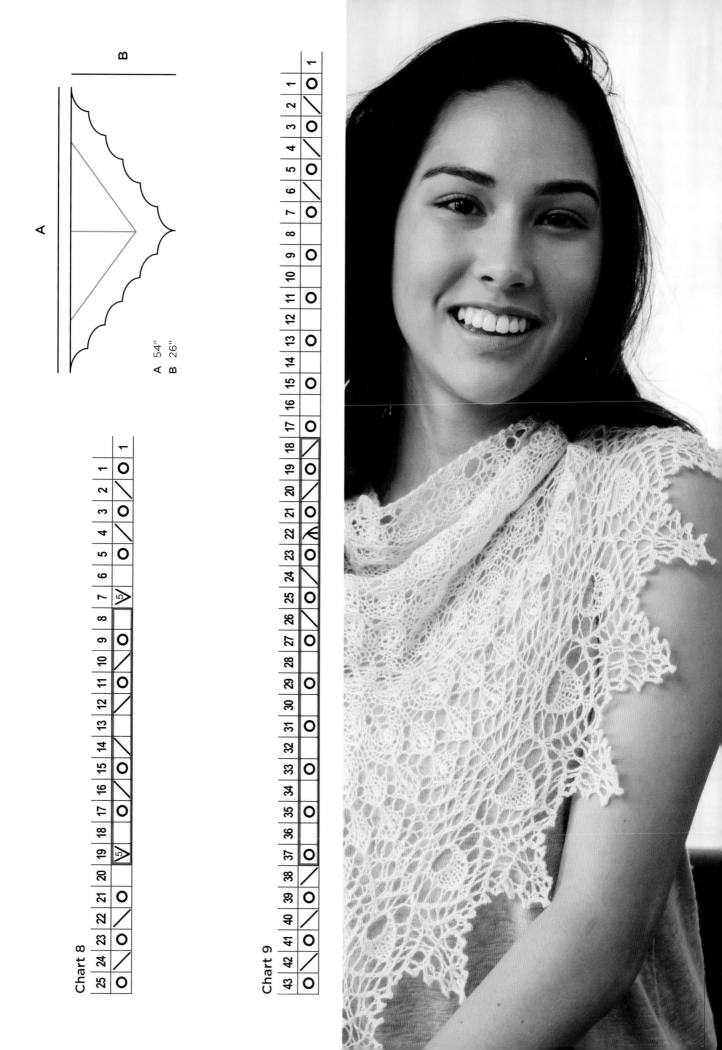

LOTUS LACE CARDIGAN

by Donna Estin

FINISHED MEASUREMENTS

32.25" (37.75, 41.75, 44.25, 48.25)"
finished bust measurement
Garment is meant to be worn with 4" of
positive ease.

YARN

Knit Picks Capretta
(80% Fine Merino Wool, 10% Cashmere,
10% Nylon; 230 yards/50g): Cream
25600, 6 (7, 8, 9, 10) balls.

NEEDLES

US 2 (3mm) 32" circular needles, or size
to obtain gauge.

NOTIONS

Yarn Needle
Stitch Markers
Scrap Yarn or Stitch Holder

GAUGE

30 sts and 42 rows = 4" over Lotus Lace,
blocked.

26 sts and 47 rows = 4" over Border
Lace, blocked.

For pattern support, contact
donnaestindesigns@gmail.com

Notes:

Lotus Lace Cardigan is an all season cardigan that can be worn over a tank top in the summer and a long sleeve tee in cooler months. The modern cut, longer length with curved front hem make this fun to wear. Sleeves are worked as an extension of the body. Worked flat from the bottom up in one piece on circular needles then divided at the armholes. Lotus Lace Cardigan has both charts and schematics.

Lengths of blocked lace will be longer than unblocked. When shaping neck and working armholes, the measurements listed are finished, blocked measurements. If your blocked row gauge is 10.5 rows per inch you can work to the number of rows as written.
The charts are read from right to left on RS rows (odd numbers), and left to right on WS rows (even numbers).

Lotus Lace Stitch Pattern (worked flat over multiples of 10 sts plus 1)

Rows 1 - 5: Knit.
Row 6 (WS): P1, *YO, P3, CDDP, P3, YO, P1; rep from * to end.
Row 7 (RS): *K2, YO, K2, CDD, K2, YO, K1; rep from * to last st, K1.
Row 8: P1, *P2, YO, P1, CDDP, P1, YO, P3; rep from * to end.
Row 9: *K4, YO, CDD, YO, K3; rep from * to last st, K1.
Row 10: P1, *P1, K2, P3, K2, P2; rep from * to end.
Row 11: *K1, YO, Ssk, P1, YO, CDD, YO, P1, K2tog, YO; rep from * to last st, K1.
Row 12: P1, *P2, (K1, P3) twice; rep from * to end.
Row 13: *K2, YO, Ssk, YO, CDD, YO, K2tog, YO, K1; rep from * to last st, K1.
Row 14: P1, *P1, K1, P5, K1, P2; rep from * to end.
Row 15: *K2, P1, K1, YO, CDD, YO, K1, P1, K1; rep from * to last st, K1.
Row 16: P1, *P1, K1, P5, K1, P2; rep from * to end.
Rep Rows 1-16 for pattern.

Border Lace Stitch Pattern (worked flat over multiples of 6 sts plus 1)

Row 1 (RS): K1, *YO, Ssk, K1, K2tog, YO, K1; rep from * to end.
Row 2 (WS): P2, YO, P3tog, YO, P1; rep from * to last st, P1.
Row 3: Knit.
Row 4: *P1, P2tog TBL, YO, P1, YO, P2tog; rep from * to last st, P1.
Row 5: K2tog, *YO, K3, YO, Sk2p; rep to last 5 sts, YO, K3, YO, Ssk.
Row 6: Purl.
Rep Rows 1-6 for pattern.

Garter Stitch
All Rows: Knit.

Centered Double Decrease (CDD) RS: Sl first and 2nd sts tog K-wise, K1, pass 2 slipped sts over the K st. 2 sts dec.

Centered Double Decrease Purl (CDDP) WS: Insert needle into the back loops of the
2nd then first sts (as if to P-TBL) but slip these 2 tog instead, P1, pass 2 slipped
sts over the P st. 2 sts dec.

DIRECTIONS

Body

It's helpful to circle the YO/dec pairs and always work them together when shaping. If you don't have enough sts to work the pair, work in St st (K on RS, P on WS) instead.

Loosely CO 165 (205, 235, 235, 265) sts. Begin with a RS row, work 2 rows in Garter st.

Next Row (RS): K1, begin Row 1 of Lotus Lace Chart, working 10-st rep 16 (20, 23, 23, 26) times, work to end of chart, K1. Maintain the first and last st of each row in St st for selvedges, cont to work Lotus Lace Chart through Row 16 then work Rows 1-16 1 (1, 1, 2, 2) more times. 205 (245, 275, 295, 325) sts.

Next Row (RS): K2, work center sts 12-22, working the 10-st rep 20 (24, 27, 29, 32) times, K2. Without increasing, cont as established, maintain the first and last 2 sts of each row in St st until piece measures 20" or 210 rows (13 repeats of Lotus Lace Chart plus first 2 Garter st rows), end with a WS row and begin neck shaping.

Neck Shaping Dec Row (RS): K1, Ssk, work in pattern to last 3 sts, K2tog, K1. 2 sts dec.

Rep Dec Row every 10th row 3 more times. 197 (237, 267, 287, 317) sts. Work next row (WS) even.

Divide for Armholes

Next Row (RS): K1, pattern across 37 (47, 57, 57, 67) sts, place sts just worked on scrap yarn for right front, pattern across 120 (140, 150, 170, 180) sts, K2tog, place st just worked and remaining 37 (47, 57, 57, 67) sts on scrap yarn for left front. Work next row (WS) even across Back sts.

Back

Next Row (RS): K1, YO, pattern across row to last st, YO, K1. 2 sts inc.

Next Row (WS): P1, YO, pattern across row to last st, YO, P1. 2 sts inc.

Rep last 2 rows 4 more times, working inc into Lotus Lace when possible. 140 (160, 170, 190, 200) sts.

Cont to work in pattern without inc until armhole opening measures 6 (6.5, 7, 7.5, 8)" or 64 (68, 74, 78, 84) rows, end with a WS row.

Shoulders

Beginning with a RS row, loosely BO 2 sts at beginning of next 10 rows. 120 (140, 150, 170, 180) sts.

BO 10 sts at beginning of next 6 (6, 8, 8, 10) rows. 60 (80, 70, 90, 80) sts.

BO 4 (12, 7, 13, 6) sts at beginning of next 2 rows. Put remaining 52 (56, 56, 64, 68) sts on scrap yarn for back neck.

Right Front

Neck and shoulder shaping occur at the same time, read through entire section before beginning.

Return 38 (48, 58, 58, 68) sts to needles and work next row (WS) even. Cont neck shaping and begin sleeve shaping:

Next Row (RS): K1, pattern across row to last st, YO, K1. 1 st inc for sleeve.

Next Row (WS): P1, YO, pattern across row to last st, P1. 1 st inc for sleeve.

Rep last 2 rows 4 more times, working inc into Lotus Lace when possible, AT THE SAME TIME, cont shaping neck by dec 1 st at beginning (K1, Ssk, pattern across row) of every 8th (6th, 3rd, 8th, 3rd) RS row 4 (6, 8, 5, 6) times then at beginning of every 8th RS row 0 (0, 3, 0, 6) times. 44 (52, 57, 63, 66) sts.

When armhole opening measures 6 (6.5, 7, 7.5, 8)" or 64 (68, 74, 78, 84) rows, end with a RS row.

Shoulder

Beginning with a WS row, loosely BO 2 sts at beginning of every WS row 5 times. 34 (42, 47, 53, 56) sts.

BO 10 sts at beginning of every WS row 2 (3, 4, 4, 5) times.

BO remaining 14 (12, 7, 13, 6) sts at beginning of next WS row.

Left Front

Neck and shoulder shaping occur at the same time, read through entire section before beginning.

Return 38 (48, 58, 58, 68) sts to needles. Cont neck shaping and begin sleeve shaping:

Next Row (RS): K1, YO, pattern across row to last st, K1. 1 st inc for sleeve.

Next Row (WS): P1, pattern across row to last st, YO, P1. 1 st inc for sleeve.

Rep last 2 rows 4 more times, working inc into Lotus Lace when possible, AT THE SAME TIME, cont shaping neck by dec 1 st at the end (pattern across to last 3 sts, K2tog, K1) of every 8th (6th, 3rd, 8th, 3rd) RS row 4 (6, 8, 5, 6) times, then at the end of every 8th RS row 0 (0, 3, 0, 6) times. 44 (52, 57, 63, 66) sts.

When armhole opening measures same as right front, end with a WS row.

Shoulder

Beginning with a RS row, loosely BO 2 sts at beginning of every RS row 5 times. 34 (42, 47, 53, 56) sts.

BO 10 sts at beginning of every RS row 2 (3, 4, 4, 5) times.

BO remaining 14 (12, 7, 13, 6) sts at beginning of next RS row.

Finishing

Sew shoulder seams. With RS facing, begin at underarm and PU 90 (97, 105, 112, 120) sts along sleeve cuff. Beginning with a WS row, work 2 rows in Garter st. On a WS row loosely BO all sts K-wise. Sew sleeve seam. Rep for other side.

Neckband

With RS facing, start at bottom of right front and PU 158 (158, 160, 161, 163) sts to armholes, 58 (60, 62, 68, 71) sts to shoulder, PM, place 52 (56, 56, 64, 68) held back neck sts onto needle, PM, PU 58 (60, 62, 68, 71) sts to left front armholes, 158 (158, 160, 161, 163) sts to bottom of left front. 484 (492, 500, 522, 536) sts.

Work first and last 5 sts of each row of Neckband very loosely.

Next Row (WS): K1, P1, K1, P213 (215, 219, 226, 231), SM, dec 3 (5, 1, 5, 1) sts evenly between markers, SM, (49 (51, 55, 59, 67) sts remain between markers), P213 (215, 219, 226, 231), K1, P1, K1. 481 (487, 499, 517, 535) sts.

Next Row (RS): Removing markers as you go, K1, P1, K1, work Row 1 of Border Lace, working the 6-st rep 79 (80, 82, 85, 88) times, work to end of chart, K1, P1, K1.

Next Row (WS): K1, P1, K1, P2tog, work next row of Border Lace until 5 sts remain, Ssp, K1, P1, K1. 2 sts dec.

Next Row (RS): K1, P1, K1, Ssk, work next row of Border Lace until 5 sts remain, K2tog, K1, P1, K1. 2 sts dec.

Cont working last 2 rows, dec 1 st at beginning and end of each row and working all rows of Border Lace Chart, rep Rows 1-6 until neckband measures 2.5". Loosely BO all sts.

Weave in yarn tails. Block to measurements. Block border lace above the bottom curve flat. Stretch the bottom section along the curve into a diagonal line, allowing the border lace to bunch together.

Lotus Lace Chart

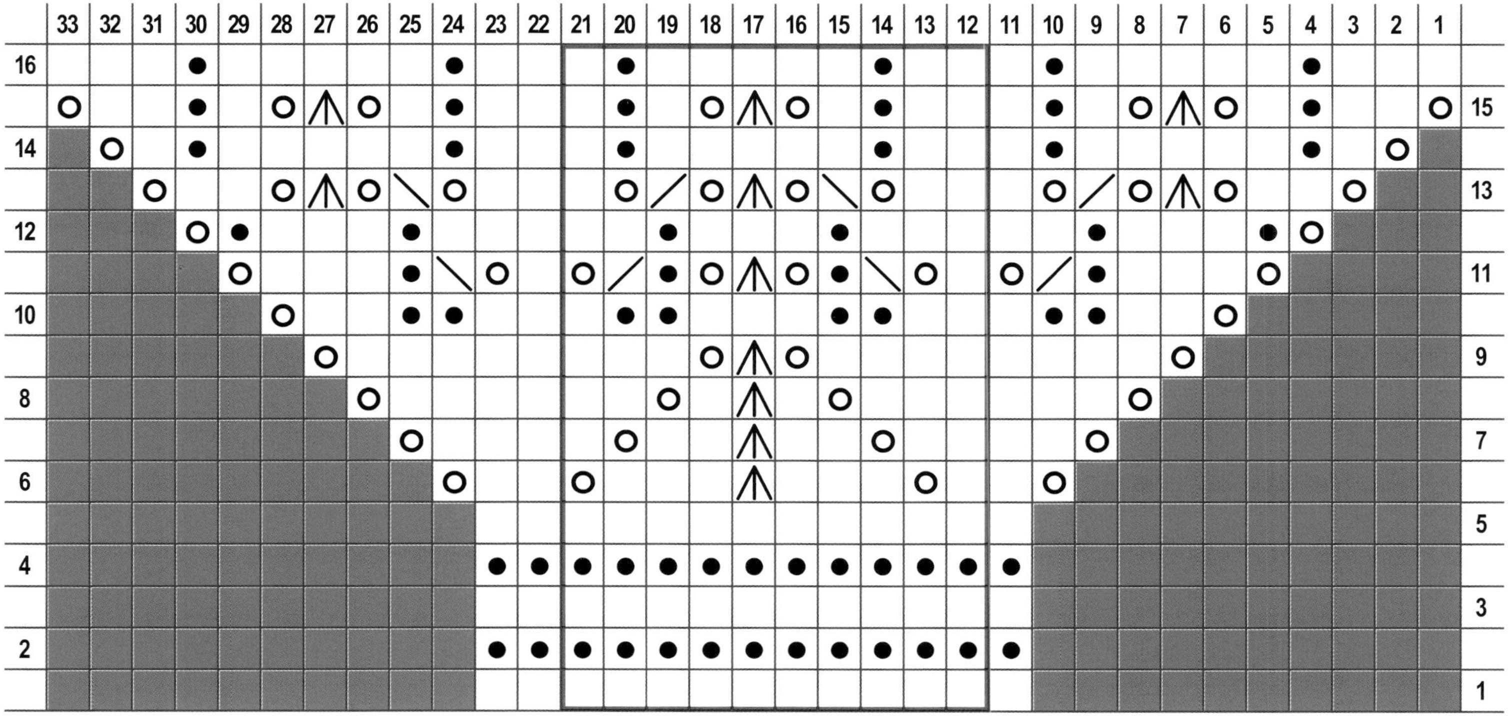

Legend

K
RS: Knit stitch
WS: Purl stitch

P
● RS: Purl stitch
WS: Knit stitch

YO
O Yarn Over

K2tog
RS: Knit 2 stitches together as 1 stitch.
WS: Purl 2 stitches together as 1 stitch.

SSK
RS: Slip 1 stitch as if to knit. Slip another stitch as if to knit. Insert LH needle into front of these 2 stitches and knit them together.
WS: Purl 2 stitches together in back loops, inserting needle from the left, behind and into the backs of the second and first stitches in that order.

K3tog
RS: Knit three stitches together as one.
WS: Purl three stitches together as one.

sl1 K2tog PSSO (SK2P)
Slip 1 stitch. K2tog then pass the slipped stitch over.

Central Double Dec
RS: Slip first and second stitches together as if to knit. Knit 1 stitch. Pass two slipped stitches over the knit stitch.
WS: Slip first and second stitches together as if to purl through the back loop. Purl 1 stitch. Pass two slipped stitches over the purl stitch.

No Stitch

Pattern Repeat

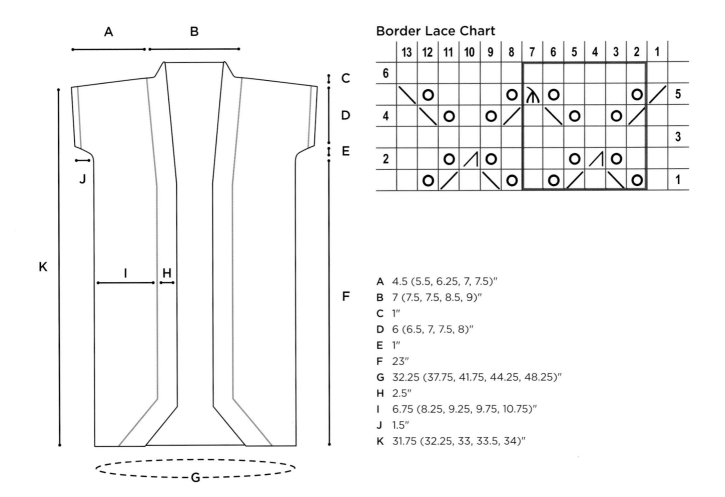

Border Lace Chart

A 4.5 (5.5, 6.25, 7, 7.5)"
B 7 (7.5, 7.5, 8.5, 9)"
C 1"
D 6 (6.5, 7, 7.5, 8)"
E 1"
F 23"
G 32.25 (37.75, 41.75, 44.25, 48.25)"
H 2.5"
I 6.75 (8.25, 9.25, 9.75, 10.75)"
J 1.5"
K 31.75 (32.25, 33, 33.5, 34)"

LYRATA STOLE

by Joyce Fassbender

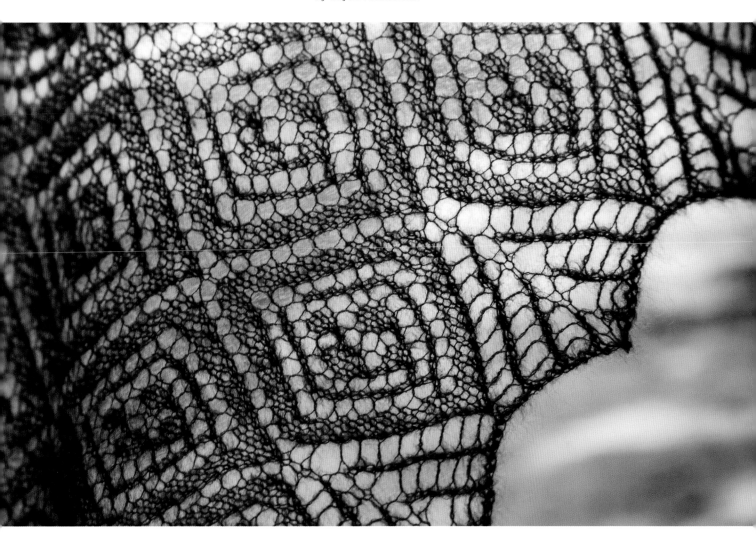

FINISHED MEASUREMENTS
80" L x 31" W

YARN
Knit Picks Aloft
(72% Super Kid Mohair, 28% Silk; 260
yards/25g): Eggplant 25210, 7 balls.

NEEDLES
US 5 (3.75mm) 32" circular needles,
or size to obtain gauge.

NOTIONS
Yarn Needle
Stitch Markers
Smooth Scrap Yarn
Size F (3.75mm) Crochet Hook
Blocking Pins or Wires

GAUGE
22 sts and 27 rows = 4" over lace
patterns, blocked.

Notes:

This rectangular stole is worked from a provisional cast on at the center back to the ends. One half is constructed first, the provisional cast on removed from the scrap yarn, and then the second half is worked from these live stitches. The vertical edges of the piece are in garter stitch lace that is worked as you go.

In order to increase the length of the project work additional repeats of Charts 1 or 3. Each additional repeat of Chart 1 will add 3" to the length; each additional repeat of Chart 3 will add 6" to the length.

Use stitch markers between pattern repeats as necessary. Placement of stitch markers between stitch pattern repeats may need to be adjusted between charts. Boxed area of charts represents pattern repeat across rows. See chart instructions for additional information.

Provisional Cast On (Crochet Chain Method)

With the crochet hook, use scrap yarn to make a slipknot and chain the number sts of the CO plus a few extra sts. Hold knitting needle in right hand. Insert the tip of your knitting needle into the first bump of the crochet chain. Wrap the project yarn around your needle as if to knit and pull the yarn through the crochet chain forming your first st. Rep this process until you have CO the correct number of sts. To unravel (when sts need to be picked up), unravel the chain, leaving live sts. Place these sts onto a knitting needle as you unravel the crochet chain.

K2tog Bind Off

K2, Sl both sts onto left needle, K2tog TBL, *K1, Sl st onto left needle, K2tog TBL; rep from * until all sts are bound off.

DIRECTIONS

For all charts: Odd (RS) rows are worked from right to left. Even (WS) rows are worked from left to right.

Side 1

CO 171 sts using Provisional Cast On. Turn work. Work WS set up row: K8, P to last 8 sts, K8.

Work Chart 1 Rows 1-20 seven times. Rep the boxed st pattern 13 times per row.
Work Chart 2 Rows 1-20 one time. Rep the boxed st pattern 6 times per row. Move st markers between st pattern repeats one st to the left on Rows 13 and 19.
Work Chart 3 Rows 1-40 two times. Rep the boxed st pattern 6 times per row. Move st markers between st pattern repeats one st to the left on Rows 17, 27, 31, and 39.
Work Chart 4 Rows 1-20 one time. Rep the boxed st pattern 6 times per row.

Side 2

After Chart 4, BO using K2tog Bind Off. Remove provisional cast on and place 171 live sts onto the needles. With WS facing you, attach yarn to first st on right end of row. Work one WS row as: K8, P to last 8 sts, K8. Rep instructions for Side 1.

Finishing

Weave in ends, wash and block.

Chart 1

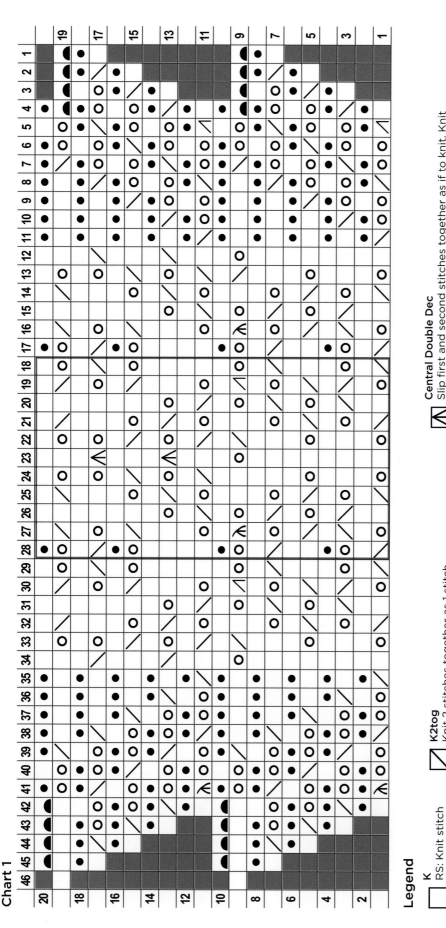

Legend

K
RS: Knit stitch
WS: Purl stitch

P
● RS: Purl stitch
WS: Knit stitch

YO
○ Yarn Over

■ No Stitch

□ Pattern Repeat

K2tog
Knit 2 stitches together as 1 stitch.

SSK
Slip 1 stitch as if to knit. Slip another stitch as if to knit.
Insert LH needle into front of these 2 stitches and knit
them together.

K3tog
Knit three stitches together as one.

Bind Off Stitch

Central Double Dec
Slip first and second stitches together as if if to knit. Knit
one stitch. Pass two slipped stitches over the knit stitch.

sl1 K2tog PSSO (SK2P)
Slip 1 stitch. K2tog then pass the slipped stitch over.

sl3 K2tog P3SSO
Slip 3 stitches. K2tog, then pass the 3 slipped stitches
over the K2tog stitch.

Chart 2

Chart 3

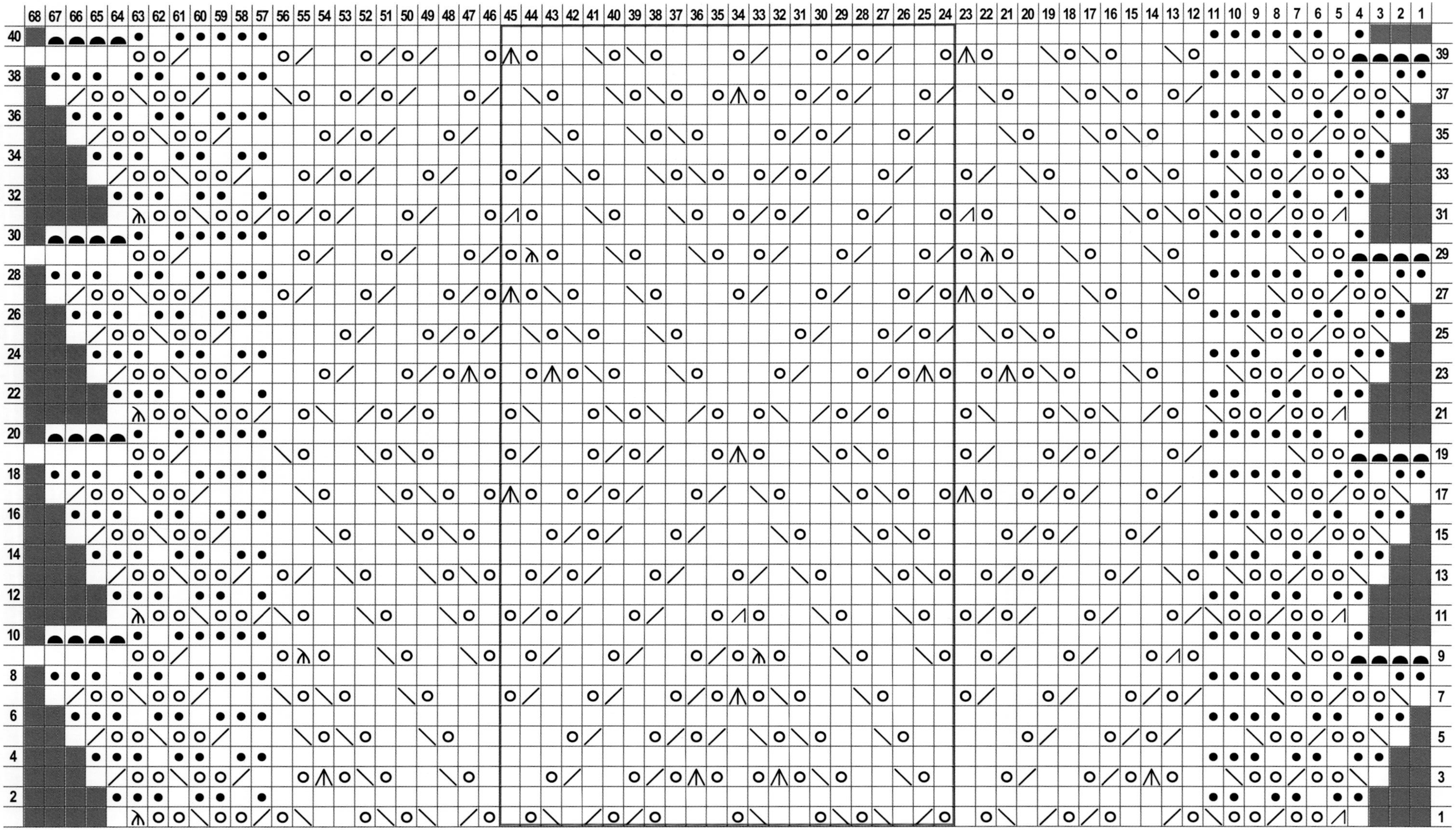

Chart 4

OPAL DAWN

by Carolyn Macpherson

FINISHED MEASUREMENTS
29.5" x 60"

YARN
Knit Picks Alpaca Cloud Lace
(100% Baby Alpaca; 440 yards/50g):
Augusta 26796, Charlotte 26766, 4
skeins each.

NEEDLES
US 2 (3mm) straight or circular needles,
or size to obtain gauge.

NOTIONS
Stitch Markers (optional)
Cable Needle
Yarn Needle
8 7/16" (11mm) buttons (optional)
Blocking Pins or Wires

GAUGE
26 sts and 40 rows = 4" over lace
patterns with yarn held double, blocked

Notes:

A quiet land is embraced by silent mist, while the pearly dawn light filters through gentle ethereal tendrils. The opal tranquility of daybreak is often fleeting, yet this skin-soft, oh-so-light, 100% baby alpaca yarn allows yourself to embrace the essence of peaceful stillness whenever you wish.

The Opal Dawn wrap measures a sensuous 29 1/2" in width and 60" in length. Marrying several lace knitting traditions, the wrap is worked flat from the short end, with pattern stitches on both right and wrong sides.

The luxurious size is ideal to wear as an elegant stole, but the pattern itself is asymmetrical, with a border appearing on only one end, and the optional addition of small buttons placed along the neck edge will allow the wearer to fasten the stole as a wrap.

Charts are read from right to left on RS rows (odd numbers) and left to right on WS rows (even numbers). The Center Panel Chart is split across two pages.

Nupp: K into st on LH needle, (loosely YO and K into the same st again) 3 times. 6 sts inc, 7 sts total. On the following row you will K7tog TBL, closing the nupp.

2/2 LC: Sl 2 sts to CN, hold in front; K2, K2 from CN.

Central Double Decrease (CDD): Sl 2 sts tog as if to K, K1; pass the two slipped sts over the st just knit. 2 sts dec.

Border (worked flat over 164 sts)

On RS rows Sl sts P-wise.

Row 1 (RS): Sl1 WYIF, P2, K2tog, YO, K1, YO, SSK, P2, *K1, YO, K5, K2tog, K1, SSK, K5, YO; rep from * 9 times, P2, K2tog, YO, K1, YO, SSK, P3.

Rows 2, 4 (WS): Sl1, K2, P5, K2, P144, K2, P5, K3.

Row 3: Sl1 WYIF, P2, K2tog, YO, K1, YO, SSK, P2, *K2, YO, K4, K2tog, K1, SSK, K4, YO, K1; rep from * 9 times, P2, K2tog, YO, K1, YO, SSK, P3.

Row 5: Sl1 WYIF, P2, K2tog, YO, K1, YO, SSK, P2, *nupp, K2, YO, K3, K2tog, K1, SSK, K3, YO, K2; rep from * 9 times, K2tog, YO, K1, YO, SSK, P3.

Row 6: Sl1, K2, P5, K2, *P15, K7tog TBL; rep from * 9 times, K2, P5, K3.

Row 7: Sl1 WYIF, P2, K2tog, YO, K1, YO, SSK, P2, *K1, nupp, K2, YO, K2, K2tog, K1, SSK, K2, YO, K2, nupp; rep from * 9 times, P2, K2tog, YO, K1, YO, SSK, P3.

Row 8: Sl1, K2, P5, K2, *K7tog TBL, P13, K7tog TBL, P1; rep from * 9 times, K2, P5, K3.

Row 9: Sl1 WYIF, P2, K2tog, YO, K1, YO, SSK, P2, *K2, nupp, K2, YO, K1, K2tog, K1, SSK, K1, YO, K2, nupp, K1; rep from * 9 times, P2, K2tog, YO, K1, YO, SSK, P3.

Row 10: Sl1, K2, P5, K2, *P1, K7tog TBL, P11, K7tog TBL, P2; rep from * 9 times, K2, P5, K3.

Row 11: Sl1 WYIF, P2, K2tog, YO, K1, YO, SSK, P2, *K3, nupp, K2, YO, K2tog, K1, SSK, YO, K2, nupp, K2; rep from * 9 times, P2, K2tog, YO, K1, YO, SSK, P3.

Row 12: Sl1, K2, P5, K2, *P2, K7tog TBL, P9, K7tog TBL, P3; rep from * 9 times, K2, P5, K3.

Row 13: Sl1 WYIF, P2, K2tog, YO, K1, YO, SSK, P2, *K4, nupp, K2, YO, CDD, YO, K2, nupp, K3; rep from * 9 times, P2, K2tog, YO, K1, YO, SSK, P3.

Row 14: Sl1, K2, P5, K2, *P3, K7tog TBL, P7, K7tog TBL, P4; rep from * 9 times, K2, P5, K3.

Row 15: Sl1 WYIF, P2, K2tog, YO, K1, YO, SSK, P2, *K1, YO, SSK, K2, nupp, K5, nupp, K2, K2tog, YO; rep from * 9 times, P2, K2tog, YO, K1, YO, SSK, P3.

Row 16: Sl1, K2, P5, K2, *P4, (K7tog TBL, P5) x 2; rep from * 9 times, K2, P5, K3.

Row 17: Sl1 WYIF, P2, K2tog, YO, K, YO, SSK, P2, *K2, YO, SSK, K2, nupp, K3, nupp, K2, K2tog, YO, K1; rep from * 9 times, P2, K2tog, YO, K1, YO, SSK, P3.

Row 18: Sl1, K2, P5, K2, *P5, K7tog TBL, P3, K7tog TBL, P6; rep from* 9 times, K2, P5, K3.

Row 19: Sl1 WYIF, P2, K2tog, YO, K1, YO, SSK, P2, *K1, (YO, SSK) x 2, K2, nupp, K1, nupp, K2, (K2tog, YO) x 2; rep from * 9 times, P2, K2tog, YO, K1, YO, SSK, P3.

Row 20: Sl1, K2, P5, K2, *P6, K7tog TBL, P1, K7tog TBL, P7; rep from * 9 times, K2, P5, K3.

Row 21: Sl1 WYIF, P2, K2tog, YO, K1, YO, SSK, P2, *K2, (YO, SSK) x 2, K2, nupp, K2, (K2tog, YO) x 2, K1; rep from * 9 times, P2, K2tog, YO, K1, YO, SSK, P3.

Row 22: Sl1, K2, P5, K2, *P7, K7tog TBL, P8; rep from * 9 times, K2, P5, K3.

Row 23: Sl1 WYIF, P2, K2tog, YO, K1, YO, SSK, P2, *K1, (YO, SSK) x 3, K3, (K2tog, YO) x 3; rep from * 9 times, P2, K2tog, YO, K1, YO, SSK, P3.

Rows 24, 26, 28: Sl1, K2, P5, K2, P144, K2, P5, K3.

Row 25: Sl1 WYIF, P2, K2tog, YO, K1, YO, SSK, P2, *K2, (YO, SSK) x 3, K1, (K2tog, YO) x 3, K1; rep from * 9 times, P2, K2tog, YO, K1, YO, SSK, P3.

Row 27: Sl1 WYIF, P2, K2tog, YO, K1, YO, SSK, P2, *K1, (YO, SSK) x 3, YO, CDD, (YO, K2tog) x 3, YO; rep from * 9 times, P2, K2tog, YO, K1, YO, SSK, P3.

Lace & Cables (worked flat over 164 sts)
On RS rows Sl sts P-wise.

Row 1 (RS): Sl1 WYIF, P2, K2tog, YO, K1, YO, SSK, P2, *P1, K4, P1, (SSK, YO) 3 times; rep from * 12 times, P2, K2tog, YO, K1, YO, SSK, P3.

Rows 2, 4, 6, 8 (WS): Sl1, K2, P5, K2, *P6, K1, P4, K1; rep from * 12 times, K2, P5, K3.

Row 3: Sl1 WYIF, P2, K2tog, YO, K1, YO, SSK, P2, *P1, K4, P1, (YO, K2tog) 3 times; rep from * 12 times, P2, K2tog, YO, K1, YO, SSK, P3.

Row 5: Sl1 WYIF, P2, K2tog, YO, K1, YO, SSK, P2, *P1, 2/2 LC, P1, (SSK, YO) 3 times; rep from * 12 times, P2, K2tog, YO, K1, YO, SSK, P3.

Row 7: Rep Row 3.

Row 9: Sl1 WYIF, P2, K2tog, YO, K1, YO, SSK, P2, *(SSK, YO) 6 times; rep from * 12 times, P2, K2tog, YO, K1, YO, SSK, P3.

Row 10: Sl1, K2, P5, K2, P144, K2, P5, K3.

Row 11: Sl1 WYIF, P2, K2tog, YO, K1, YO, SSK, P2, *(YO, K2tog) 3 times, P1, K4, P1; rep from * 12 times, P2, K2tog, YO, K1, YO, SSK, P3.

Rows 12, 14, 16, 18: Sl1, K2, P5, K2, *K1, P4, K1, P6; rep from * 12 times, K2, P5, K3.

Row 13: Sl1 WYIF, P2, K2tog, YO, K1, YO, SSK, P2, *(SSK, YO) 3 times, P1, K4, P1; rep from * 12 times, P2, K2tog, YO, K1, YO, SSK, P3.

Row 15: Sl1 WYIF, P2, K2tog, YO, K1, YO, SSK, P2, *(YO, K2tog) 3 times, P1, 2/2 LC, P1; rep from * 12 times, P2, K2tog, YO, K1, YO, SSK, P3.

Row 17: Rep Row 13.

Row 19: Sl1 WYIF, P2, K2tog, YO, K1, YO, SSK, P2, *(YO, K2tog) 6 times; rep from * 12 times, P2, K2tog, YO, K1, YO, SSK, P3.

Row 20: Rep Row 10.

Center Panel (worked flat over 164 sts)

On RS rows Sl sts P-wise.

Row 1 (RS): Sl1 WYIF, P2, K2tog, YO, K1, YO, SSK, P2, *P1, K4, P1, (SSK, YO) 3 times, K7, nupp, K9, nupp, K6, P1, K4, P1, (SSK, YO) 3 times; rep from * 3 times, P2, K2tog, YO, K1, YO, SSK, P3.

Row 2 (WS): Sl1, K2, P5, K2, *P6, K1, P4, K1, P6, K7tog TBL, P9, K7tog TBL, P13, K1, P4, K1; rep from * 3 times, K2, P5, K3.

Row 3: Sl1 WYIF, P2, K2tog, YO, K1, YO, SSK, P2, *P1, K4, P1, (YO, K2tog) 3 times, (K7, nupp x 2) twice, K6, P1, K4, P1, (YO, K2tog) 3 times; rep from * 3 times, P2, K2tog, YO, K1, YO, SSK, P3.

Row 4: Sl1, K2, P5, K2, *P6, K1, P4, K1, P6, (K7tog TBL) twice, P7, (K7tog TBL) twice, P13, K1, P4, K1; rep from * 3 times, K2, P5, K3.

Row 5: Sl1 WYIF, P2, K2tog, YO, K1, YO, SSK, P2, *P1, 2/2 LC, P1, (SSK, YO) 3 times, K7, nupp, K1, nupp, K5, nupp, K1, nupp, K6, P1, 2/2 LC, P1, (SSK, YO) 3 times; rep from * 3 times, P2, K2tog, YO, K1, YO, SSK, P3.

Row 6: Sl1, K2, P5, K2, *P6, K1, P4, K1, P6, K7tog TBL, P1, K7tog TBL, P5, K7tog TBL, P1, K7tog TBL, P13, K1, P4, K1; rep from * 3 times, K2, P5, K3.

Row 7: Sl1 WYIF, P2, K2tog, YO, K1, YO, SSK, P2, *P1, K4, P1, (YO, K2tog) 3 times, K4, (nupp) 3 times, K1, YO, SSK, nupp, K3, nupp, K2tog, YO, K1, (nupp) 3 times, K3, P1, K4, P1, (YO, K2tog) 3 times; rep from * 3 times, P2, K2tog, YO, K1, YO, SSK, P3.

Row 8: Sl1, K2, P5, K2, *P6, K1, P4, K1, P3, (K7tog TBL) 3 times, (P3, K7tog TBL) twice, P3, (K7tog TBL) 3 times, P10, K1, P4, K1; rep from * 3 times, K2, P5, K3.

Row 9: Sl1 WYIF, P2, K2tog, YO, K1, YO, SSK, P2, *(SSK, YO) 6 times, K5, nupp, K1, (YO, SSK) twice, nupp, K1, nupp, (K2tog, YO) twice, K1, nupp, K4, (SSK, YO) 6 times; rep from * 3 times, P2, K2tog, YO, K1, YO, SSK, P3.

Row 10: Sl1, K2, P5, K2, *P16, K7tog TBL, P5, K7tog TBL, P1, K7tog TBL, P5, K7tog TBL, P17; rep from * 3 times, K2, P5, K3.

Row 11: Sl1 WYIF, P2, K2tog, YO, K1, YO, SSK, P2, *(YO, K2tog) 3 times, P1, K4, P1, K6, nupp, K1, (YO, SSK) twice, nupp, (K2tog, YO) twice, K1, nupp, K5, (YO, K2tog) 3 times, P1, K4, P1; rep from * 3 times, P2, K2tog, YO, K1, YO, SSK, P3.

Row 12: Sl1, K2, P5, K2, *K1, P4, K1, P11, (K7tog TBL, P5) twice, K7tog TBL, P6, K1, P4, K1, P6; rep from * 3 times, K2, P5, K3.

Row 13: Sl1 WYIF, P2, K2tog, YO, K1, YO, SSK, P2, *(SSK, YO) 3 times, P1, K4, P1, K7, nupp, K1, YO, SSK, YO, CDD, YO, K2tog, YO, K1, nupp, K6, (SSK, YO) 3 times, P1, K4, P1; rep from * 3 times, P2, K2tog, YO, K1, YO, SSK, P3.

Row 14: Sl1, K2, P5, K2, *K1, P4, K1, P12, K7tog TBL, P9, K7tog TBL, P7, K1, P4, K1, P6; rep from * 3 times, K2, P5, K3.

Row 15: Sl1 WYIF, P2, K2tog, YO, K1, YO, SSK, P2, *(YO, K2tog) 3 times, P1, 2/2 LC, P1, K8, nupp, K1, YO, SSK, K1, K2tog, YO, K1, nupp, K7, (YO, K2tog) 3 times, P1, 2/2 LC, P1; rep from * 3 times, P2, K2tog, YO, K1, YO, SSK, P3.

Row 16: Sl1, K2, P5, K2, *K1, P4, K1, P13, K7tog TBL, P7, K7tog TBL, P8, K1, P4, K1, P6; rep from * 3 times, K2, P5, K3.

Row 17: Sl1 WYIF, P2, K2tog, YO, K1, YO, SSK, P2, *(SSK, YO) 3 times, P1, K4, P1, K9, nupp, K5, nupp, K8, (SSK, YO) 3 times, P1, K4, P1; rep from * 3 times, P2, K2tog, YO, K1, YO, SSK, P3.

Row 18: Sl1, K2, P5, K2, *K1, P4, K1, P14, K7tog TBL, P5, K7tog TBL, P9, K1, P4, K1, P6; rep from * 3 times, K2, P5, K3.

Row 19: Sl1 WYIF, P2, K2tog, YO, K1, YO, SSK, P2, *(YO, K2tog) 6 times, K8, nupp, K2tog, YO, K3, YO, SSK, nupp, K7, (YO, K2tog) 6 times; rep from * 3 times, P2, K2tog, YO, K1, YO, SSK, P3.

Row 20: Sl1, K2, P5, K2, *P19, K7tog TBL, P7, K7tog TBL, P20; rep from * 3 times, K2, P5, K3.

Row 21: Sl1 WYIF, P2, K2tog, YO, K1, YO, SSK, P2, *P1, K4, P1, (SSK, YO) 3 times, K7, nupp, (K2tog, YO) twice, K1, (YO, SSK) twice, nupp, K6, P1, K4, P1, (SSK, YO) 3 times; rep from * 3 times, P2, K2tog, YO, K1, YO, SSK, P3.

Row 22: Sl1, K2, P5, K2, *P6, K1, P4, K1, P6, K7tog TBL, P9, K7tog TBL, P13, K1, P4, K1; rep from * 3 times, K2, P5, K3.

Row 23: Sl1 WYIF, P2, K2tog, YO, K1, YO, SSK, P2, *P1, K4, P1, (YO, K2tog) 3 times, K6, nupp, (K2tog, YO) twice, K1, nupp, K1, (YO, SSK) twice, nupp, K5, P1, K4, P1, (YO, K2tog) 3 times; rep from * 3 times, P2, K2tog, YO, K1, YO, SSK, P3.

Row 24: Sl1, K2, P5, K2, *P6, K1, P4, K1, (P5, K7tog TBL) 3 times, P12, K1, P4, K1; rep from * 3 times, K2, P5, K3.

Row 25: Sl1 WYIF, P2, K2tog, YO, K1, YO, SSK, P2, *P1, 2/2 LC, P1, (SSK, YO) 3 times, K5, nupp, (K2tog, YO) twice, (K1, nupp) twice, K1, (YO, SSK) twice, nupp, K4, P1, 2/2 LC, P1, (SSK, YO) 3 times; rep from * 3 times, P2, K2tog, YO, K1, YO, SSK, P3.

Row 26: Sl1, K2, P5, K2, *P6, (K1, P4) twice, K7tog TBL, P5, K7tog TBL, P1, K7tog TBL, P5, K7tog TBL, P11, K1, P4, K1; rep from * 3 times, K2, P5, K3.

Row 27: Sl1 WYIF, P2, K2tog, YO, K1, YO, SSK, P2, *P1, K4, P1, (YO, K2tog) 3 times, K4, (nupp) 3 times, K2tog, YO, K1, nupp, K3, nupp, K1, YO, SSK, (nupp) 3 times, K3, P1, K4, P1, (YO, K2tog) 3 times; rep from * 3 times, P2, K2tog, YO, K1, YO, SSK, P3.

Row 28: Sl1, K2, P5, K2, *P6, K1, P4, K1, P3, (K7tog TBL) 3 times, (P3, K7tog TBL) twice, P3, (K7tog TBL) 3 times, P10, K1, P4, K1; rep from * 3 times, K2, P5, K3.

Row 29: Sl1 WYIF, P2, K2tog, YO, K1, YO, SSK, P2, *(SSK, YO) 6 times, K7, nupp, K1, nupp, K5, nupp, K1, nupp, K6, (SSK, YO) 6 times; rep from * 3 times, P2, K2tog, YO, K1, YO, SSK, P3.

Row 30: Sl1, K2, P5, K2, *P18, K7tog TBL, P1, K7tog TBL, P5, K7tog TBL, P1, K7tog TBL, P19; rep from * 3 times, K2, P5, K3.

Row 31: Sl1 WYIF, P2, K2tog, YO, K1, YO, SSK, P2, *(YO, K2tog) 3 times, P1, K4, P, (K7, [nupp] twice) twice, K6, (YO, K2tog) 3 times, P1, K4, P1; rep from * 3 times, P2, K2tog, YO, K1, YO, SSK, P3.

Row 32: Sl1, K2, P5, K2, *K1, P4, K1, P12, ([K7tog TBL] twice, P7) twice, K1, P4, K1, P6; rep from * 3 times, K2, P5, K3.

Row 33: Sl1 WYIF, P2, K2tog, YO, K1, YO, SSK, P2, *(SSK, YO) 3 times, P1, K4, P1, K7, nupp, K9, nupp, K6, (SSK, YO) 3 times, P1, K4, P1; rep from * 3 times, P2, K2tog, YO, K1, YO, SSK, P3.

Row 34: Sl1, K2, P5, K2, *P18, K7tog TBL, P9, K7tog TBL, P19; rep from * 3 times, K2, P5, K3.

Row 35: Sl1 WYIF, P2, K2tog, YO, K1, YO, SSK, P2, *K6, nupp, K9, nupp, K15, nupp, K9, nupp, K5; rep from * 3 times, P2, K2tog, YO, K1, YO, SSK, P3.

Row 36: Sl1, K2, P5, K2, *P5, K7tog TBL, P9, K7tog TBL, P15, K7tog TBL, P9, K7tog TBL, P6; rep from * 3 times, K2, P5, K3.

Row 37: Sl1 WYIF, P2, K2tog, YO, K1, YO, SSK, P2, *K6, (nupp) twice, K7, (nupp) twice, K15, (nupp) twice, K7, (nupp) twice, K5; rep from * 3 times, P2, K2tog, YO, K1, YO, SSK, P3.

Row 38: Sl1, K2, P5, K2, *P5, (K7tog TBL) twice, P7, (K7tog TBL) twice, P15, (K7tog TBL) twice, P7, (K7tog TBL) twice, P6; rep from * 3 times, K2, P5, K3.

Row 39: Sl1 WYIF, P2, K2tog, YO, K1, YO, SSK, P2, *K6, nupp, K1, nupp, K5, nupp, K1, nupp, K15, (nupp, K1, nupp, K5) twice; rep from * 3 times, P2, K2tog, YO, K1, YO, SSK, P3.

Row 40: Sl1, K2, P5, K2, *(P5, K7tog TBL, P1, K7tog TBL) twice, P15, K7tog TBL, P1, K7tog TBL, P5, K7tog TBL, P1, K7tog TBL, P6; rep from * 3 times, K2, P5, K3.

Row 41: Sl1 WYIF, P2, K2tog, YO, K1, YO, SSK, P2, *K3, (nupp) 3 times, K1, YO, SSK, nupp, K3, nupp, K2tog, YO, K1, (nupp) 3 times, K9, (nupp) 3 times, K1, YO, SSK, nupp, K3, nupp, K2tog, YO, K1, (nupp) 3 times, K2; rep from * 3 times, P2, K2tog, YO, K1, YO, SSK, P3.

Row 42: Sl1, K2, P5, K2, *P2, (K7tog TBL) 3 times, (P3, K7tog TBL) twice, P3, (K7tog TBL) 3 times, P9, (K7tog TBL) 3 times, (P3, K7tog TBL) twice, P3, (K7tog TBL) 3 times, P3; rep from * 3 times, K2, P5, K3.

Row 43: Sl1 WYIF, P2, K2tog, YO, K1, YO, SSK, P2, *K4, nupp, K1, (YO, SSK) twice, nupp, K1, nupp, (K2tog, YO) twice, K1, nupp, K11, nupp, K1, (YO, SSK) twice, nupp, K1, nupp, (K2tog, YO) twice, K1, nupp, K3; rep from * 3 times, P2, K2tog, YO, K1, YO, SSK, P3.

Row 44: Sl1, K2, P5, K2, *P3, K7tog TBL, P5, K7tog TBL, P1, K7tog TBL, P5, K7tog TBL, P11, K7tog TBL, P5, K7tog TBL, P1, K7tog TBL, P5, K7tog TBL, P4; rep from * 3 times, K2, P5, K3.

Row 45: Sl1 WYIF, P2, K2tog, YO, K1, YO, SSK, P2, *K5, nupp, K1, (YO, SSK) twice, nupp, (K2tog, YO) twice, K1, nupp, K13, nupp, K1, (YO, SSK) twice, nupp, (K2tog, YO) twice, K1, nupp, K4; rep from * 3 times, P2, K2tog, YO, K1, YO, SSK, P3.

Row 46: Sl1, K2, P5, K2, *P4, (K7tog TBL, P5) twice, K7tog TBL, P13, (K7tog TBL, P5) 3 times; rep from * 3 times, K2, P5, K3.

Row 47: Sl1 WYIF, P2, K2tog, YO, K1, YO, SSK, P2, *K6, nupp, K1, YO, SSK, YO, CDD, YO, K2tog, YO, K1, nupp, K15, nupp, K1, YO, SSK, YO, CDD, YO, K2tog, YO, K1, nupp, K5; rep from * 3 times, P2, K2tog, YO, K1, YO, SSK, P3.

Row 48: Sl1, K2, P5, K2, *P5, K7tog TBL, P9, K7tog TBL, P15, K7tog TBL, P9, K7tog TBL, P6; rep from * 3 times, K2, P5, K3.

Row 49: Sl1 WYIF, P2, K2tog, YO, K1, YO, SSK, P2, *K7, nupp, K1, YO, SSK, K1, K2tog, YO, K1, nupp, K17, nupp, K1, YO, SSK, K1, K2tog, YO, K1, nupp, K6; rep from * 3 times, P2, K2tog, YO, K1, YO, SSK, P3.

Row 50: Sl1, K2, P5, K2, *P6, K7tog TBL, P7, K7tog TBL, P17, (K7tog TBL, P7) twice; rep from * 3 times, K2, P5, K3.

Row 51: Sl1 WYIF, P2, K2tog, YO, K1, YO, SSK, P2, *K8, nupp, K5, nupp, K19, nupp, K5, nupp, K7; rep from * 3 times, P2, K2tog, YO, K1, YO, SSK, P3.

Row 52: Sl1, K2, P5, K2, *P7, K7tog TBL, P5, K7tog TBL, P19, K7tog TBL, P5, K7tog TBL, P8; rep from * 3 times, K2, P5, K3.

Row 53: Sl1 WYIF, P2, K2tog, YO, K1, YO, SSK, P2, *K7, nupp, K2tog, YO, K3, YO, SSK, nupp, K17, nupp, K2tog, YO, K3, YO, SSK, nupp, K6; rep from * 3 times, P2, K2tog, YO, K1, YO, SSK, P3.

Row 54: Sl1, K2, P5, K2, *P6, K7tog TBL, P7, K7tog TBL, P17, (K7tog TBL, P7) twice; rep from * 3 times, K2, P5, K3.

Row 55: Sl1 WYIF, P2, K2tog, YO, K1, YO, SSK, P2, *K6, nupp, (K2tog, YO) twice, K1, (YO, SSK) twice, nupp, K15, nupp, (K2tog, YO) twice, K1, (YO, SSK) twice, nupp, K5; rep from * 3 times, P2, K2tog, YO, K1, YO, SSK, P3.

Row 56: Sl1, K2, P5, K2, *P5, K7tog TBL, P9, K7tog TBL, P15, K7tog TBL, P9, K7tog TBL, P6; rep from * 3 times, K2, P5, K3.

Row 57: Sl1 WYIF, P2, K2tog, YO, K1, YO, SSK, P2, *K5, nupp, (K2tog, YO) twice, K1, nupp, K1, (YO, SSK) twice, nupp, K13, nupp, (K2tog, YO) twice, K1, nupp, K1, (YO, SSK) twice, nupp, K4; rep from * 3 times, P2, K2tog, YO, K1, YO, SSK, P3.

Row 58: Sl1, K2, P5, K2, *P4, (K7tog TBL, P5) twice, K7tog TBL, P13, (K7tog TBL, P5) 3 times; rep from * 3 times, K2, P5, K3.

Row 59: Sl1 WYIF, P2, K2tog, YO, K1, YO, SSK, P2, *K4, nupp, (K2tog, YO) twice, (K1, nupp) twice, K1, (YO, SSK) twice, nupp, K11, nupp, (K2tog, YO) twice, (K1, nupp) twice, K1, (YO, SSK) twice, nupp, K3; rep from * 3 times, P2, K2tog, YO, K1, YO, SSK, P3.

Row 60: Sl1, K2, P5, K2, *P3, K7tog TBL, P5, K7tog TBL, P1, K7tog TBL, P5, K7tog TBL, P11, K7tog TBL, P5, K7tog TBL, P1, K7tog TBL, P5, K7tog TBL, P4; rep from * 3 times, K2, P5, K3.

Row 61: Sl1 WYIF, P2, K2tog, YO, K1, YO, SSK, P2, *K3, (nupp) 3 times, K2tog, YO, K1, nupp, K3, nupp, K1, YO, SSK, (nupp) 3 times, K9, (nupp) 3 times, K2tog, YO, K1, nupp, K3, nupp, K1, YO, SSK, (nupp) 3 times, K2; rep from * 3 times, P2, K2tog, YO, K1, YO, SSK, P3.

Row 62: Sl1, K2, P5, K2, *P2, (K7tog TBL) 3 times, (P3, K7tog TBL) twice, P3, (K7tog TBL) 3 times, P9, (K7tog TBL) 3 times, (P3, K7tog TBL) twice, P3, (K7tog TBL) 3 times, P3; rep from * 3 times, K2, P5, K3.

Row 63: Sl1 WYIF, P2, K2tog, YO, K1, YO, SSK, P2, *K6, nupp, K1, nupp, K5, nupp, K1, nupp, K15, (nupp, K1, nupp, K5) twice; rep from * 3 times, P2, K2tog, YO, K1, YO, SSK, P3.

Row 64: Sl1, K2, P5, K2, *(P5, K7tog TBL, P1, K7tog TBL) twice, P15, K7tog TBL, P1, K7tog TBL, P5, K7tog TBL, P1, K7tog TBL, P6; rep from * 3 times, K2, P5, K3.

Row 65: Sl1 WYIF, P2, K2tog, YO, K1, YO, SSK, P2, *K6, (nupp) twice, K7, (nupp) twice, K15, (nupp) twice, K7, (nupp) twice, K5; rep from * 3 times, P2, K2tog, YO, K1, YO, SSK, P3.

Row 66: Sl1, K2, P5, k2, *P5, (K7tog TBL) twice, P7, (K7tog TBL) twice, P15, (K7tog TBL) twice, P7, (K7tog TBL) twice, P6; rep from * 3 times, K2, P5, K3.

Row 67: Sl1 WYIF, P2, K2tog, YO, K1, YO, SSK, P2, *K6, nupp, K9, nupp, K15, nupp, K9, nupp, K5; rep from * 3 times, P2, K2tog, YO, K1, YO, SSK, P3.

Row 68: Sl1, K2, P5, K2, *P5, K7tog TBL, P9, K7tog TBL, P15, K7tog TBL, P9, K7tog TBL, P6; rep from * 3 times, K2, P5, K3.

DIRECTIONS

With yarn held double throughout (1 strand of each color), CO 164 sts.

Row 1 (RS): Sl1 WYIF, K to last st, P1.
Row 2 (WS): Sl1, P to end of row.

Work Rows 1-28 of the Border chart.

Row 1 (RS): Sl1 WYIF, P2, K2tog, YO, K1, YO, SSK, P2, *YO, K2tog; rep from * 72 times, P2, K2tog, YO, K1, YO, SSK, P3.
Row 2 (WS): Sl1, K2, P5, K2, P144, K2, P5, K3.

Work Rows 1-20 of the Lace & Cables chart, 8 times.

Work Rows 1-68 of the Center Panel chart, 2 times.

Work Rows 1-33 of the Center Panel chart.

Set-up Row (WS): Sl1 WYIF, K2, P5, K2, *K1, P4, K1, P12, K7tog TBL, P9, K7tog TBL, P7, K1, P4, K1, P6; rep from * 3 times, K2, P5, K3.

Work Rows 15-20 of the Lace & Cables chart.

Work Rows 1-20 of the Lace & Cables chart, 10 times.

BO all sts.

Finishing

Weave in ends, soak and block to measurements.

Optional Buttons

Fold the wrap in half width-wise so that the wrong sides are touching. Along the upper edge, from the fold, leave 14" for neck. Then using pins, along the back right side edge, mark out the equal placement for 8 buttons (approximately 1 button every 2").
Sew on buttons. Use the eyelets along the front right side edge as button holes.

Border Chart

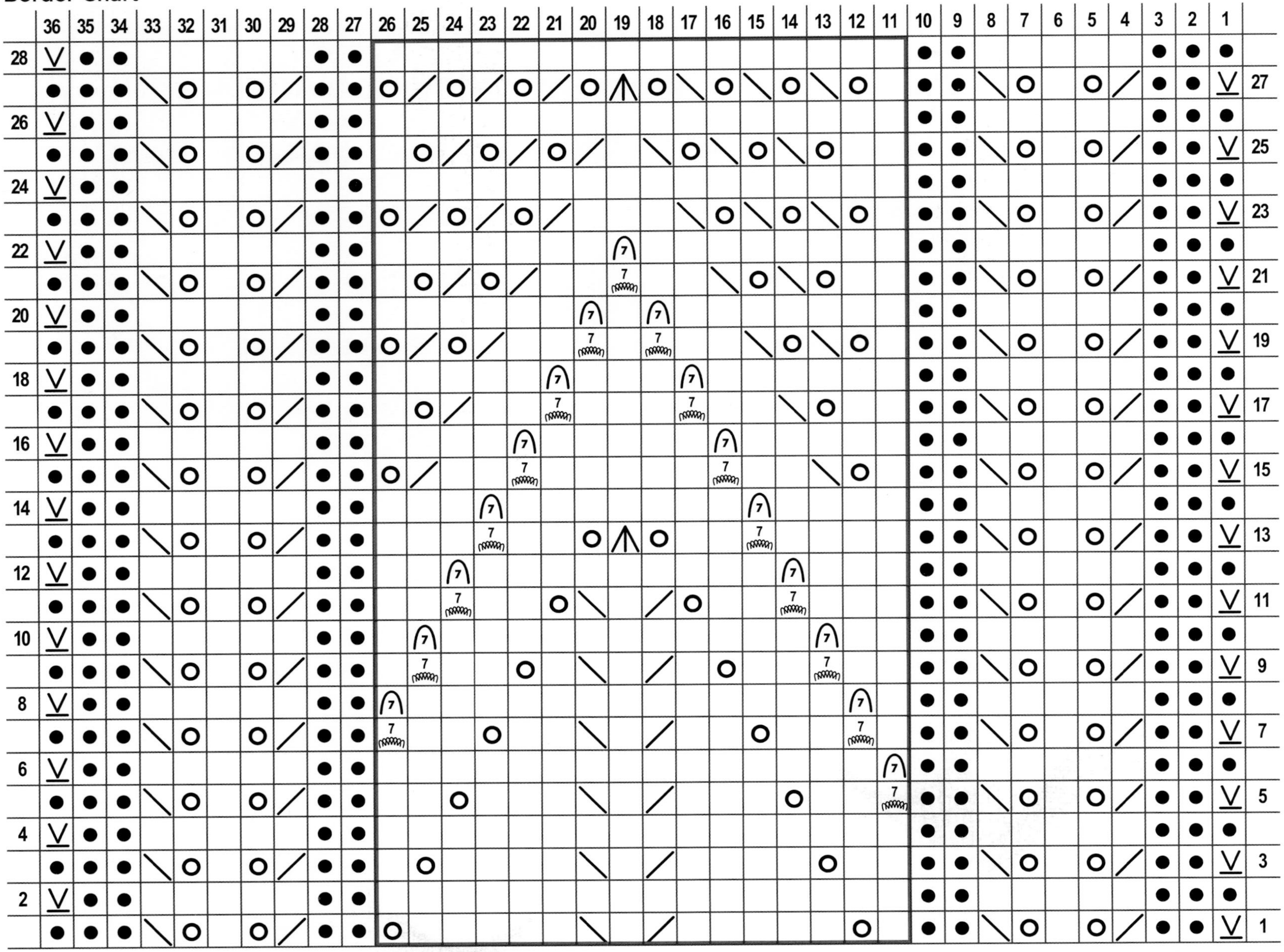

Note: The legend for this chart is located on the following page.

Lace & Cables Chart

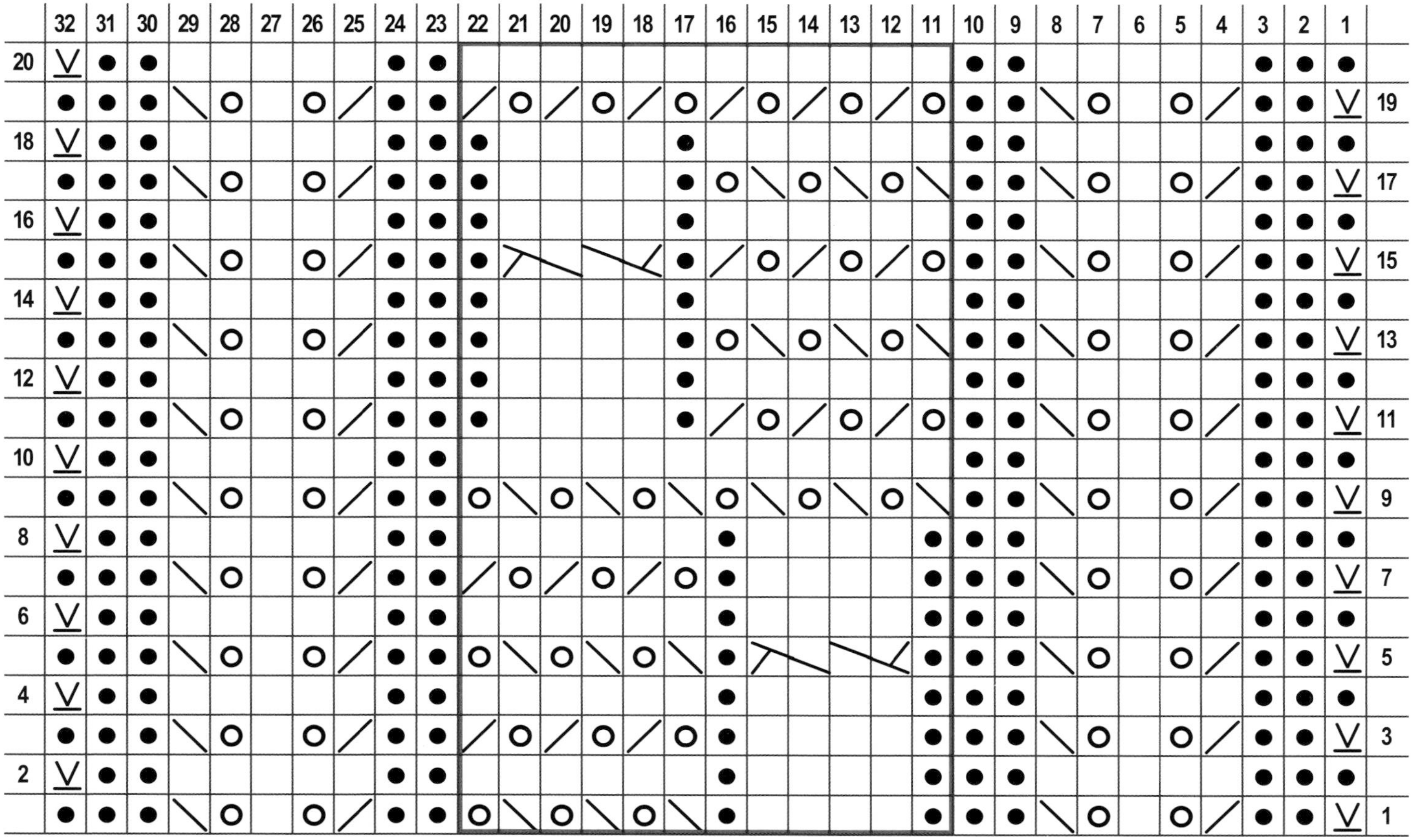

Legend

K
RS: Knit stitch
WS: Purl stitch

P
RS: Purl stitch
WS: Knit stitch

YO
Yarn Over

Pattern Repeat

K2tog
Knit 2 stitches together as 1 stitch.

SSK
Slip 1 stitch as if to knit. Slip another stitch as if to knit.
Insert LH needle into front of these 2 stitches and knit
them together.

Slip WYIF
Slip stitch as if to purl with yarn in front.

Central Double Dec
Slip first and second stitches together as if to knit. Knit
one stitch. Pass two slipped stitches over the knit stitch.

K7tog TBL
RS: Knit 7 stitches together in back loops as one.
WS: Purl 7 stitches together as one, inserting needle
from the left and behind.

7-Stitch Nupp
On the RS loosely work (K, YO, K, YO, K, YO, K) into 1
stitch. On the next WS row purl all 7 stitches together.
1 stitch remains.

C2 Over 2 Left
Sl2 to CN, hold in front. K2, K2 from CN.

Center Panel Chart

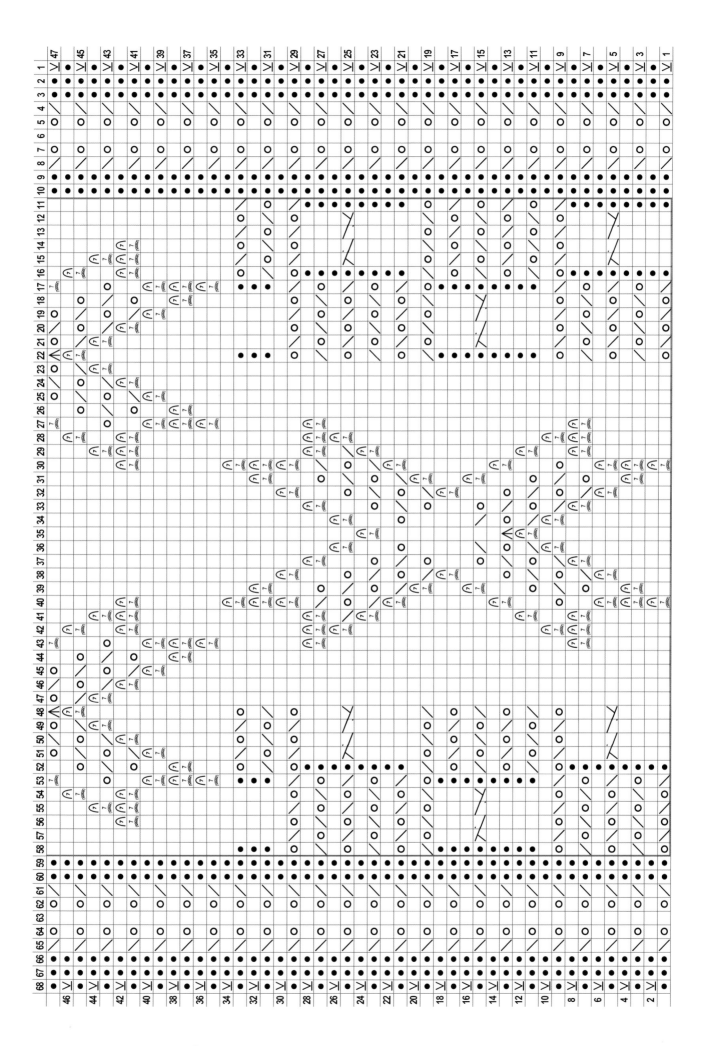

ORNAMENTAL PARASOLS

by Helen Metcalfe

FINISHED MEASUREMENTS

31.75" (34.75, 38, 41, 46.75, 50, 53, 58.75, 62)'' finished bust measurement, buttoned.
Garment is meant to be worn with 0-2" of ease.

YARN

Knit Picks Capretta
(80% Fine Merino Wool, 10% Cashmere, 10% Nylon; 230 yards/50g): Sagebrush 26563, 6 (6, 7, 7, 8, 9, 9, 10, 11) balls.

NEEDLES

US 2 (3mm) straight or circular needles, or size to obtain gauge.

NOTIONS

Stitch Holder
8" (8, 8, 8, 8, 8, 9, 9, 9) 0.75" Buttons
Yarn Needle

GAUGE

24 sts and 39 rows = 4" in Ornamental Parasols Pattern, blocked.
26 sts and 39 rows = 4" in St st, blocked.

Notes:

This cardigan is knitted flat from the bottom up, in one piece to the armholes where the fronts and back are worked separately. Featuring set in sleeves with a garter stitch trim as a finish.

I wanted this intricate stitch structure to take center stage in this lightweight cardigan. The gorgeous Capretta gives beautiful definition to this complex lace knit.

Note that stitches should only be counted after the 5th, 6th, 11th, 12th, 13th, 14th, 19th, 20th, 25th, 26th, 27th and 28th rows. The chart is read from right to left on RS rows (odd numbers, and left to right on WS rows (even numbers).

SKP: SL1, K1, pass slipped st over. 1 st dec.

Ornamental Parasols Stitch Pattern (worked flat over multiples of 18 sts plus 1)

Row 1 (RS): K1, *(P2, K1) twice, YO, K2tog, YO, K1, YO, SKP, YO, K1, (P2, K1) twice; rep from * to end. 2 sts inc.

Row 2 (WS): *(P1, K2) twice, P9, K2, P1, K2; rep from * to last st, P1.

Row 3: K1, *(P2, K1) twice, YO, K2tog, YO, K3, YO, SKP, YO, K1, (P2, K1) twice, K1; rep from * to end. 2 sts inc.

Row 4: *(P1, K2) twice, P11, K2, P1, K2; rep from * to last st, P1.

Row 5: K1, *(P2tog, K1) twice, YO, K2tog, YO, SKP, K1, K2tog, YO, SKP, YO, K1, (P2tog, K1) twice; rep from * to end. 4 sts dec.

Row 6: *(P1, K1) twice, P11, K1, P1, K1; rep from * to last st, P1.

Row 7: K1, *(P1, K1) twice, YO, K2tog, YO, K1 TBL, YO, Sk2p, YO, K1 TBL, YO, SKP, YO, (K1, P1) twice, K1; rep from * to end. 2 sts inc.

Row 8: *(P1, K1) twice, P13, K1, P1, K1; rep from * to last st, P1.

Row 9: K1, *K2tog twice, YO, K2tog, YO, K3, YO, K1, YO, K3, (YO, SKP) twice, SKP, K1; rep from * to end.

Rows 10, 12, 14: Purl.

Row 11: K1, *(K2tog, YO) twice, SKP, K1, K2tog, YO, K1, YO, SKP, K1, K2tog, (YO, SKP) twice, K1; rep from * to end. 2 sts dec.

Row 13: K2tog, *YO, K2tog, YO, K1 TBL, YO, Sk2p, YO, K3, YO, Sk2p, YO, K1 TBL, YO, SKP, YO, Sk2p; rep from * to end, replacing the last Sk2p in the last rep with SKP.

Row 15: K1, *YO, SKP, YO, K1, (P2, K1) 4 times, YO, K2tog, YO, K1; rep from * to end. 2 sts inc.

Row 16: *P5, (K2, P1) 3 times, K2, P4; rep from * to last st, P1.

Row 17: K2, YO, SKP, YO, K1, (P2, K1) 4 times, YO, K2tog, *YO, K3, YO, SKP, YO, K1, (P2, K1) 4 times YO, K2tog; rep from * to last 2 sts, YO, K2. 2 sts inc.

Row 18: *P6, K2, (P1, K2) 3 times, P5; rep from * to last st, P1.

Row 19: K1, *K2tog, YO, SKP, YO, (K1, P2tog) 4 times, K1, YO, K2tog, YO, SKP, K1; rep from * to end. 4 sts dec.

Row 20: *P6, K1, (P1, K1) 3 times, P5; rep from * to last st, P1.

Row 21: K2tog, *YO, K1 TBL, YO, SKP, YO, K1, (P1, K1) 4 times, YO, K2tog, YO, K1 TBL, YO, Sk2p; rep from * to end, replacing the last Sk2p in the last rep with SKP. 2 sts inc.

Row 22: *P7, K1, (P1, K1) 3 times, P6; rep from * to last st, P1.

Row 23: K1, *YO, K3, (YO, SKP) twice, SKP, K1, K2tog, (K2tog, YO) twice, K3, YO, K1; rep from * to end.

Rows 24, 26, 28: Purl.

Row 25: K1, *YO, SKP, K1, K2tog, (YO, SKP) twice, K1, (K2tog, YO) twice, SKP, K1, K2tog, YO, K1; rep from * to end. 2 sts dec.

Row 27: K2, YO, Sk2p, YO, K1 TBL, YO, SKP, YO, Sk2p, YO, K2tog, YO, K1 TBL, YO, Sk2p, *YO, K3, YO, Sk2p, YO, K1 TBL, YO, SKP, YO, Sk2p, YO, K2tog, YO, K1 TBL, YO, Sk2p; rep from * to last 2 sts, YO, K2.

Rep Rows 1-28 for pattern.

DIRECTIONS

Body

The body is worked flat in one piece until the armholes, then the fronts and back are worked separately.

Hem

CO 185 (203, 223, 241, 275, 295, 313, 347, 367) sts. Knit 6 rows.

Commence Ornamental Parasols Stitch Pattern.
Row 1 (RS): K2 (2, 3, 3, 2, 3, 3, 2, 3), work Row 1 of Ornamental Parasols Stitch Pattern from chart or written instructions until 2 (2, 3, 3, 2, 3, 3, 2, 3) sts remain, K to end.
Row 2 (WS): P2 (2, 3, 3, 2, 3, 3, 2, 3), work row 2 of Ornamental Parasols Stitch Pattern from chart or written instructions until 2 (2, 3, 3, 2, 3, 3, 2, 3) sts remain, P to end.
Rep these two rows continuing to follow Ornamental Parasols Stitch Pattern from chart or written instructions until piece measures 13.25" from bottom edge, finishing after pattern Row 12.

As armhole and neckband shaping progresses the lace reps will be interrupted. As you cont to follow chart/written instructions, note that st counts differ from row to row dependent on position within ornamental parasols pattern. Due to placement of increases and decreases, where there are partial reps throughout the pattern, given st counts assume that the chart has been followed to either a full rep or halfway across a rep (either st 23 or 12). All excess partial rep sts are knit on a RS row and purled on a WS row.
For pattern Rows 7 and 27, substitute Sk2p positioned at st 12 with a K2tog when completing a partial rep.

Right Front

PM after st 44 (47, 51, 54, 62, 66, 70, 78, 83), now working these sts only, placing remaining 141 (156, 172, 187, 213, 229, 243, 269, 284) sts on hold.
Row 1 (RS): K2 (2, 3, 3, 2, 3, 3, 2, 3), work 2 (2, 2.5, 2.5, 3, 3, 3.5, 4, 4) reps of chart, K to M. 44 (47, 51, 54, 62, 66, 70, 78, 83) sts.
Maintain pattern for 1 (1, 2, 2, 2, 2, 2, 2, 2) more rows.
Maintaining pattern, at beginning of next - (-, 1, 2, 3, 4, 4, 5, 5) WS rows BO as follows;
BO - (-, 2, 3, 4, 5, 5, 6, 6) sts 1 time.
BO - (-, -, 2, 3, 4, 4, 5, 5) sts 1 time.
BO - (-, -, -, 2, 3, 3, 4, 4) sts 1 time.
BO - (-, -, -, -, 2, 2, 3, 3) sts 1 time.
BO - (-, -, -, -, -, -, 2, 2) sts 1 time. 44 (47, 54, 59, 53, 57, 61, 64, 69) sts
Dec Row (RS): Maintain pattern to last 3 sts, K2tog, K1.
1 st dec.
Next Row (WS): Maintain pattern.
Rep the last 2 rows 5 (5, 4, 2, 3, 1, 3, 2, 7) more times. 38 (41, 44, 50, 49, 50, 57, 60, 55) sts.
38 (41, 44, 46, 49, 50, 52, 55, 55) sts after next rep of Row 5, 11, 13, 19, 25 and 27.
Cont without shaping until work measures 17.75 (18, 18.75, 19.25, 19.75, 20.25, 20.75, 21.25, 21.75)" from CO edge, ending after WS pattern row 28 (2, 10, 14, 20, 24, 2, 6, 12).

Neck Band Shaping

Next Row (RS): BO 9 (11, 12, 12, 14, 14, 14, 14, 15) sts, maintain pattern to end.
Next Row: Maintain pattern.
Neckband Dec Row (RS): K1, SSK, maintain pattern to end. 1 st dec.
Rep the last 2 rows 8 (7, 9, 10, 9, 10, 11, 12, 11) more times.
Maintain pattern without shaping until work measures 20.75 (21, 21.75, 22.25, 22.75, 23.25, 23.75, 24.25, 24.75)" from CO edge finishing after WS chart Row 28 (2, 10, 14, 20, 24, 2, 6, 12). 20 (24, 24, 23, 25, 27, 28, 28, 28) sts.

Shoulder Shaping

Now working in St st (K on RS, P on WS), BO 5 (6, 6, 6, 6, 7, 7, 7, 7) sts at the beginning of the next 3 WS rows.
Work 1 RS row.
BO 5 (6, 6, 5, 7, 6, 7, 7, 7) remaining sts.

Back

Return 93 (105, 115, 125, 141, 151, 161, 177, 187) sts to working needle, leaving 48 (51, 57, 62, 72, 78, 82, 92, 97) sts on hold.

Next Row (RS): BO 4 (4, 6, 8, 10, 12, 12, 14, 14) sts, not including st on RH needle after BO, K7 (4, 8, 3, 1, 6, 1, 9, 5), starting with chart st 1 (1, 1, 1, 1, 14, 1, 14, 14) work Row 13 of Ornamental Parasols chart until last 8 (5, -, 4, 2, 5, 2, 8, 4) sts, K to end. 89 (101, 109, 117, 131, 139, 149, 163, 173) sts
Maintaining pattern work 1 WS row.

BO - (-, 2, 3, 4, 5, 5, 6, 6) sts at beginning of next - (-, 2, 2, 2, 2, 2, 2, 2) rows.

BO - (-, -, 2, 3, 4, 4, 5, 5) sts at beginning of next - (-, -, 2, 2, 2, 2, 2, 2) rows.

BO - (-, -, -, 2, 3, 3, 4, 4) sts at beginning of next - (-, -, -, 2, 2, 2, 2, 2) rows.

BO - (-, -, -, -, 2, 2, 3, 3) sts at beginning of next - (-, -, -, -, 2, 2, 2, 2) rows.

BO - (-, -, -, -, -, -, 2, 2) sts at beginning of next - (-, -, -, -, -, -, 2, 2) rows.

Dec Row (RS): K1, Ssk, maintain pattern to last 3 sts, K2tog, K1. 2 sts dec.

Rep Dec Row every RS row 5 (5, 4, 2, 3, 1, 3, 2, 7) more times. St count after next rep of row 5 (11, 13, 19, 25, 27) is 77 (89, 95, 101, 105, 107, 113, 117, 117) sts.

Maintain pattern without shaping until work measures 20.75 (21, 21.75, 22.25, 22.75, 23.25, 23.75, 24.25, 24.75)" from CO edge finishing after WS chart Row 28 (2, 10, 14, 20, 24, 2, 6, 12).

Shoulder Shaping

BO 5 (6, 6, 6, 6, 7, 7, 7, 7) sts at beginning of next 6 rows.
BO 5 (6, 6, 5, 7, 6, 7, 7, 7) sts at beginning of next 2 rows.
BO remaining sts.

Left Front

Return remaining 48 (51, 57, 62, 72, 78, 82, 92, 97) sts to working needle.

Next Row (RS): BO 4 (4, 6, 8, 10, 12, 12, 14, 14) sts, not including st on RH needle after BO, K4 (7, 2, 5, 4, 7, 3, 2, 6), starting with chart st 1 (1, 14, 14, 1, 1, 14, 1, 1) work Row 13 of Ornamental Parasols chart until 2 (2, 3, 3, 2, 3, 3, 2, 3) sts remain, K to end. 44 (47, 51, 54, 62, 66, 70, 78, 83) sts.
Work 1 WS row.

At beginning of next - (-, 1, 2, 3, 4, 4, 5, 5) RS rows BO as follows;

BO - (-, 2, 3, 4, 5, 5, 6, 6) sts 1 time.
BO - (-, -, 2, 3, 4, 4, 5, 5) sts 1 time.
BO - (-, -, -, 2, 3, 3, 4, 4) sts 1 time.
BO - (-, -, -, -, 2, 2, 3, 3) sts 1 time.
BO - (-, -, -, -, -, -, 2, 2) sts 1 time. 44 (47, 54, 59, 53, 57, 61, 64, 69) sts.
Work 1 WS row.

Dec Row (RS): K1, SSK, maintain pattern to end. 1 st dec.
Next Row (WS): Maintain pattern.
Rep the last 2 rows 5 (5, 4, 2, 3, 1, 3, 2, 7) more times. 38 (41, 44, 50, 49, 50, 57, 60, 55) sts.
38 (41, 44, 46, 49, 50, 52, 55, 55) sts after next rep of row 5, 11, 13, 19, 25 and 27.

Continue without shaping until work measures 17.75 (18, 18.75, 19.25, 19.75, 20.25, 20.75, 21.25, 21.75)" from CO edge, ending after WS pattern row 2 (4, 12, 16, 2, 8, 12, 28, 6). Work 1 more RS row.

Neckband Shaping

Next Row (WS): BO 9 (11, 12, 12, 14, 14, 14, 14, 15) sts, maintain pattern to end.
Neckband Dec Row (RS): Maintain pattern to last 3 sts, K2tog, K1. 1 st dec.
Next Row: Maintain pattern.
Rep the last 2 rows 8 (7, 9, 10, 9, 10, 11, 12, 11) more times.
Maintain pattern without shaping until work measures 20.75 (21, 21.75, 22.25, 22.75, 23.25, 23.75, 24.25, 24.75)" from CO edge finishing after WS chart Row 28 (2, 10, 14, 20, 24, 2, 6, 12). 20 (24, 24, 23, 25, 27, 28, 28, 28) sts.

Shoulder Shaping

Now working in St st, BO 5 (6, 6, 6, 6, 7, 7, 7, 7) sts at the beginning of the next 3 RS rows.
Work 1 WS row.
BO 5 (6, 6, 5, 7, 6, 7, 7, 7) remaining sts.

Sleeves

The sleeves are worked flat from the wrists up. Incorporate increased sts into lace pattern, balancing increases and decreases to avoid increasing or decreasing too many sts as the pattern progresses.

CO 57 (57, 63, 63, 71, 71, 75, 75, 79) sts. Knit 12 rows.

Row 1 (RS): K1 (1, 4, 4, 8, 8, 1, 1, 3) work chart Row 1 starting with chart st 1 to last 1 (1, 4, 4, 8, 8, 1, 1, 3) sts of row, K to end.

Row 2 (WS): P1 (1, 4, 4, 8, 8, 1, 1, 3), maintain chart pattern to last 1 (1, 4, 4, 8, 8, 1, 1, 3) sts of row, P to end.

Maintaining pattern work a further - (8, 8, 8, 4, -, 6, 6, 4) rows.

Inc Row (RS): K1, M1, maintain pattern to last st, M1, K1. 2 sts inc.

Rep Inc Row every 14 (10, 10, 8, 10, 6, 6, 4, 4) rows and every alternate - (12, 12, 10, -, 8, -, 6, 6) rows 10 (6, 6, 8, 15, 10, 22, 13, 13) times, work a further - (10, 10, -, -, -, -, -, 4) rows followed by - (1, 1, -, -, -, -, -, 1) more Inc Row.

St count after next rep of row 5 (11, 13, 19, 25, 27) is 77 (83, 89, 95, 101, 111, 119, 127, 133) sts.

Cont without shaping until work measures 16.75" from CO edge finishing after chart Row 12. (5 full chart reps, plus Rows 1-11.)

Cap Sleeve Shaping

BO 2 (2, 3, 4, 5, 6, 6, 7, 8) sts at beginning of next 2 rows.

Work 2 (2, 2, 2, -, -, -, -) rows without shaping.

Dec Row (RS): K1, SSK, maintain pattern to last 3 sts, K2tog, K1. 2 sts dec.

Next Row: Maintain pattern.

Rep the last 2 rows 21 (22, 24, 27, 28, 29, 30, 32, 33) more times.

BO 3 (3, 3, 2, 2, 3, 4, 4, 4) sts at beginning of next 2 rows.

BO 2 (3, 2, 2, 2, 3, 4, 4, 4) sts at beginning of next 2 rows.

BO remaining 21 (23, 23, 23, 27, 29, 29, 33, 37) sts.

Please note this includes an extra 2 (2, -,-, 2, 2, -, 2, 4) increased pattern sts.

Neckband

Sew shoulder seams before commencing neckband. With RS facing and starting with top right edge, PU and K34 (36, 37, 37, 39, 39, 39, 39, 40) sts evenly around right front neck, PU and K37 (41, 47, 55, 55, 53, 57, 61, 61) sts from back neck, PU and K34 (36, 37, 37, 39, 39, 39, 39, 40) sts evenly around left front neck. 105 (113, 121, 129, 133, 131, 135, 139, 141) sts.

Knit 9 rows.

BO.

Left Button Band

With RS facing and starting at neckband edge of Left Front, PU and K121 (123, 128, 131, 134, 138, 141, 144, 147) sts.

Knit 9 rows.

BO.

Right Buttonhole Band

With RS facing and starting at lower edge of Right Front, PU and K121 (123, 128, 131, 134, 138, 141, 144, 147) sts.

Knit 5 rows.

Next Row: K6 (3, 6, 4, 5, 8, 5, 6, 8), work 1 Row Buttonhole as follows; (worked over 4 sts) **Bring the yarn to the front, between the needles, SI the next st P-wise and bring the yarn to the back between the needles, wrapping the base of the st. *SI the next st P-wise and pass the first slipped st over, rep from * twice more. SI the st remaining on the RH needle to the left and turn the work. With WS facing Cable CO 4 sts. Before placing the last CO st on the LH needle, bring the yarn to the front between the needles, place the st on the LH needle and turn the work. SI the next st K-wise and pass the last CO st over it. K11 (12, 12, 13, 13, 13, 12, 12, 12); rep from ** a further 6 (6, 6, 6, 6, 6, 7, 7, 7) times. Work 1 more buttonhole, K6 (4, 6, 4, 6, 7, 4, 6, 7).

Knit 3 rows.

BO.

Finishing

Line up the center of the sleeve head with the shoulder seam, joining the seams using Mattress st. Sew sleeve seam. Rep for other sleeve. Attach buttons along left buttonband to line up with buttonholes. Weave in ends, wash and block to diagram.

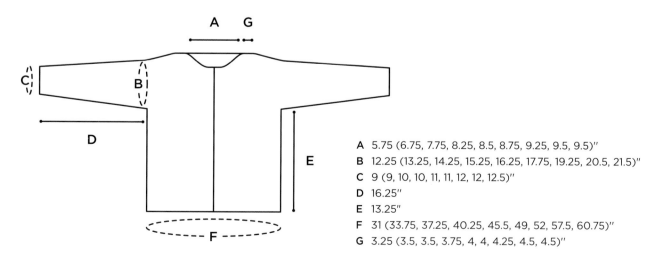

A 5.75 (6.75, 7.75, 8.25, 8.5, 8.75, 9.25, 9.5, 9.5)"

B 12.25 (13.25, 14.25, 15.25, 16.25, 17.75, 19.25, 20.5, 21.5)"

C 9 (9, 10, 10, 11, 11, 12, 12, 12.5)"

D 16.25"

E 13.25"

F 31 (33.75, 37.25, 40.25, 45.5, 49, 52, 57.5, 60.75)"

G 3.25 (3.5, 3.5, 3.75, 4, 4, 4.25, 4.5, 4.5)"

Ornamental Parasols Stitch Pattern

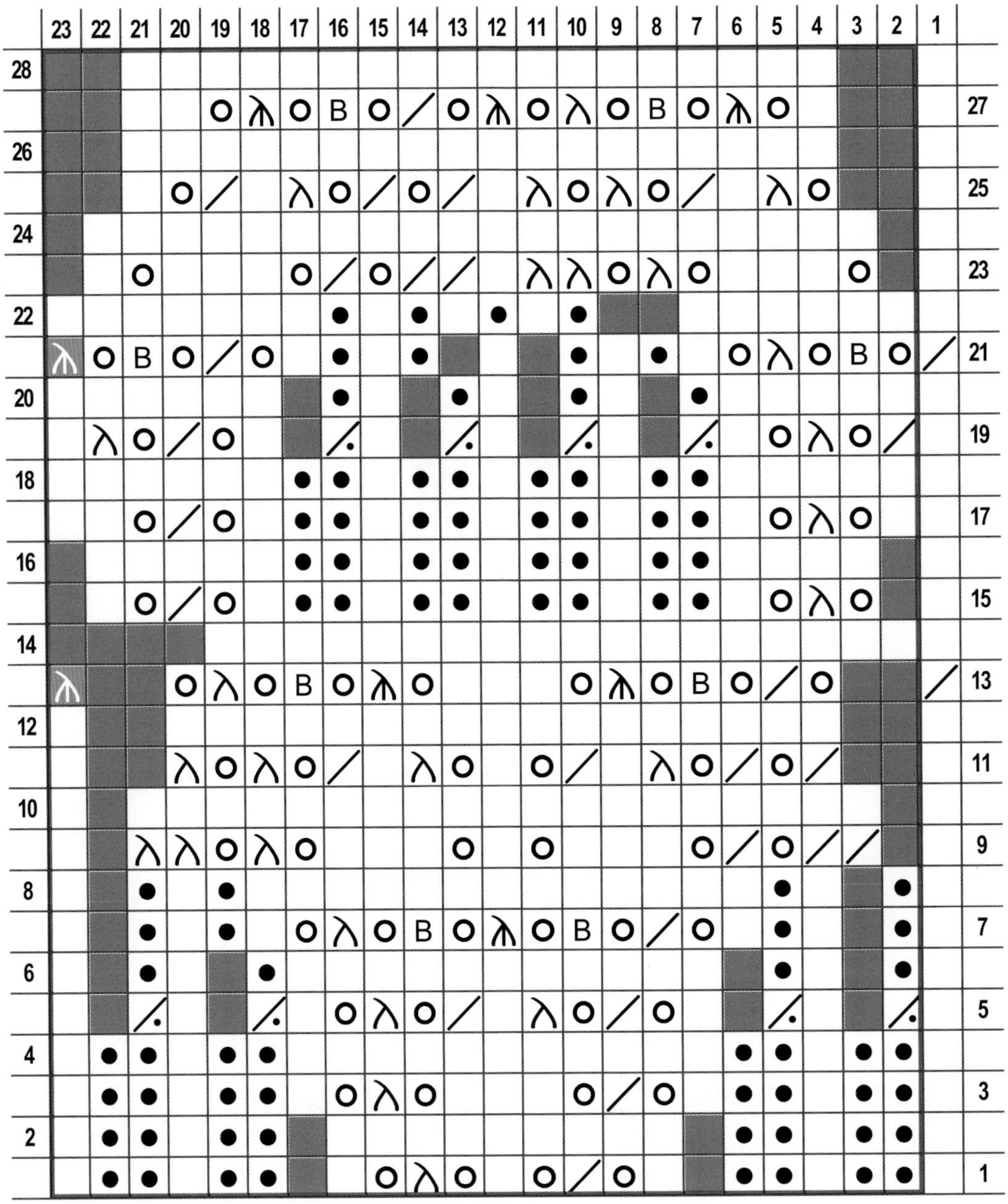

Legend

K
RS: Knit stitch
WS: Purl stitch

P
RS: Purl stitch
WS: Knit stitch

YO
Yarn Over

B
Knit TBL
Knit stitch through back loop.

K2tog
Knit 2 stitches together as 1 stitch.

P2tog
Purl two stitches together.

sl1 K1 PSSO (SKP)
Slip 1. Knit 1. Pass slipped stitch over knit stitch.

sl1 K2tog PSSO (SK2P)
Slip 1 stitch. K2tog then pass the slipped stitch over.

sl1 K2tog PSSO (SK2P)/sl1 K1 PSSO (SKP)
Replace the highlighted SK2P with a SKP when completing the last pattern repeat.

No Stitch

Pattern Repeat

RIPPLE TEE

by Jill Wright

FINISHED MEASUREMENTS

32.25" (36.25, 40.25, 44.25, 48.25, 52.25, 56.25, 60.25, 64.25)" finished bust measurement.
Garment is meant to be worn with 2" of positive ease.

YARN

Knit Picks Gloss Fingering
(70% Merino Wool, 30% Silk; 220 yards/50g): Robot 25015: 3 (4, 4, 5, 5, 5, 6, 6, 7) balls.

NEEDLES

US 4 (3.5mm) straight or circular needles, or size to obtain gauge.

NOTIONS

Yarn Needle
Stitch Holders or Scrap Yarn

GAUGE

24 sts and 34 rows = 4" over Ripple Lace Stitch Pattern, blocked.

For pattern support, contact
jill2who@gmail.com

Notes:

The simple shape of this cropped tee is a perfect canvas for the pretty ripple stitch. Carefully placed decreases and increases form points at the lower edge, the columns of lace draw flattering lines, and grafting forms comfortably stretchy shoulder seams.

The Ripple Tee is a "T" shaped cropped top worked from the bottom up with a round neck. A section of the stitch pattern has patterning worked on both right and wrong side rows. Some sizes have reverse stockinette stitch panels at side seams to preserve the lace stitch pattern integrity.

The chart is read from right to left on RS rows (even numbers), and left to right on WS rows (odd numbers).

Ripple Lace Stitch Pattern (worked flat over multiples of 18 sts plus 1)

Row 1: P1, (K8, P1) to end.
Row 2: Knit.
Row 3: P1, *(K2tog, YO) 4 times, P1, (YO, SSK) 4 times, P1; rep from * to end.
Row 4: Knit.
Row 5: P1, (K8, P1) to end.
Row 6: K1, (P8, K1) to end.
Row 7: P1, *K2tog 3 times, YO, (K1, YO) twice, P1, YO, (K1, YO) twice, SSK 3 times, P1; rep from * to end.
Row 8: K1, (P8, K1) to end.
Row 9: P1, (K8, P1) to end.
Row 10: K.
Rows 11-14: Rep Rows 3-6.
Row 15: P1, (K3, K2tog, K3, YO, P1, YO, K3, SSK, K3, P1) to end.
Row 16: K1, (P2, SSP, P3, YO, P1, K1, P1, YO, P3, P2tog, P2, K1) to end.
Row 17: P1, (K1, K2tog, K3, YO, K2, P1, K2, YO, K3, SSK, K1, P1) to end.
Row 18: K1, (SSP, P3, YO, P3, K1, P3, YO, P3, P2tog, K1) to end.
Rows 19-26: Rep Rows 15-18.
Row 27: P1, (K8, P1) to end.
Row 28: K1, (P8, K1) to end.
Rep Rows 1-28 for pattern.

Kitchener Stitch (for grafting)

With pieces to be joined on needles and needles held parallel to one another with points to the right hand side, thread yarn in yarn needle, insert as if to purl the first st on the front needle keeping st on needle, insert yarn needle as if to knit in first st on back needle, leave st on needle. *Insert yarn needle as if to knit in first st on front needle dropping st from needle, then insert as if to purl next st on front needle keeping it on needle. Insert yarn needle as if to purl in first st on back needle dropping st from needle, insert as if to knit next st on back needle keeping st on needle.* Rep from * to * until 1 st remains on each needle. Insert yarn needle as if to knit in st on front needle, drop st off needle, insert in st as if to purl on back needle, drop st off needle.

DIRECTIONS

Back

CO 99 (111, 123, 135, 147, 159, 171, 183, 195) sts.

Set-up Row 1 (RS): P 4 (1, 7, 4, 1, 7, 4, 1, 7), work Row 1 of Ripple Lace Stitch Pattern beginning at st 10 (1, 1, 10, 1, 1, 10, 1, 1) rep the st pattern 5 (6, 6, 7, 8, 8, 9, 10, 10) times ending with st 10 (19, 19, 10, 19, 19, 10, 19, 19), P4 (1, 7, 4, 1, 7, 4, 1, 7). Cont working in Ripple Lace Stitch Pattern for a total of 68 rows for all sizes, ending with Row 12.

Shape Sleeves

Next Row (RS): Loosely CO 33 (36, 39, 42, 45, 48, 48, 48, 48) sts. P1 (1, 1, 1, 1, 1, 6, 3, 1), work Row 13 of Ripple Lace Stitch Pattern beginning at st 10 (1, 10, 1, 10, 1, 1, 10, 1) working pattern rep 7 (8, 8.5, 9.5, 10.5, 11, 11.5, 12.5, 13) times, P1 (1, 1, 1, 1, 1, 6, 3, 1).

Next Row (WS): Loosely CO 33 (36, 39, 42, 45, 48, 48, 48, 48) sts. P1 (1, 1, 1, 1, 1, 6, 3, 1), work Row 14 of Ripple Lace Stitch Pattern beginning at st 10 (1, 10, 1, 10, 1, 1, 10, 1) working pattern rep 9 (10, 11, 12, 13, 14, 14, 15, 16) times, P1 (1, 1, 1, 1, 1, 6, 3, 1). 165 (183, 201, 219, 237, 255, 267, 279, 291) sts.
Continue working in Ripple Lace Stitch Pattern to 132 (136, 136, 140, 144, 144, 148, 152, 152) rows, or 15.5 (16, 16, 16.5, 17, 17, 17.5, 18, 18)". Sl 60 (69, 78, 85, 94, 103, 107, 113, 119) sts to stitch holder, Sl next 45 (45, 45, 49, 49, 49, 53, 53, 53) sts to a 2nd stitch holder for back neck, Sl remaining sts to a 3rd stitch holder.

Front

Work same as back to end of Row 116 or 13.5" (all sizes), ending with a WS row.

Shape Right Neck

Dec Row 1 (RS): Work in pattern for 65 (74, 83, 92, 101, 110, 116, 122, 128) sts, K2tog, Sl next 31 sts to stitch holder, SSK, work in pattern across. 66 (75, 84, 93, 102, 111, 117, 123, 129) sts.

Dec Row 2 (WS): Work in pattern to last 2 sts, SSP. 1 st dec. 65 (74, 83, 92, 101, 110, 116, 122, 128) sts.

Dec Row 3 (RS): SSK, work in pattern across. 1 st dec. 64 (73, 82, 91, 100, 109, 115, 121, 127) sts.
Rep last 2 rows 1 (1, 1, 2, 2, 2, 3, 3, 3) more times. 62 (71, 80, 87, 96, 105, 109, 115, 121) sts.
Work 1 WS row even.

Next Row (RS): Work Dec Row 3 omitting first YO on 3 largest sizes only. 61 (70, 79, 86, 95, 104, 108, 114, 120) sts.
Rep last 2 rows once more (all sizes). 60 (69, 78, 85, 94, 103, 107, 113, 119) sts.
Work even in pattern to shoulder until front length matches Back. Sl sts to stitch holder.

Shape Left Neck

With WS facing, join in yarn at neck edge.

Dec Row 1(WS): P2tog, pattern across. 1 st dec. 65 (74, 83, 92, 101, 110, 116, 122, 128) sts.

Dec Row 2 (RS): Pattern to last 2 sts, K2tog. 1 st dec. 64 (73, 82, 91, 100, 109, 115, 121, 127) sts.
Rep last 2 rows 1 (1, 1, 2, 2, 2, 3, 3, 3) more times. 62 (71, 80, 87, 96, 105, 109, 115, 121) sts.
Work 1 WS row even.

Next Row (RS): Work Dec Row 2 omitting last YO on 3 largest sizes only. 61 (70, 79, 86, 95, 104, 108, 114, 120) sts.
Rep last 2 rows once more (all sizes). 60 (69, 78, 85, 94, 103, 107, 113, 119) sts.
Work even in pattern to shoulder until front length matches Back. Sl sts to stitch holder.

Block Front and Back to diagram.

Finishing

Graft right shoulder.

Neckband

With RS facing, beginning at left shoulder edge, PU & K 5 (8, 8, 11, 13, 13, 15, 18, 18) sts down left neck edge, 8 (8, 8, 11, 11, 11, 14, 14, 14) sts across left neck shaping, place 31 held sts (all sizes) across front neck on needle, 8 (8, 8, 11, 11, 11, 14, 14, 14) sts up right neck shaping, 5 (8, 8, 11, 13, 13, 15, 18, 18) sts up right neck edge, place 45 (45, 45, 49, 49, 49, 53, 53, 53) held sts across back neck on needle. 102 (108, 108, 124, 128, 128, 142, 148, 148) sts.

Purl 3 rows. Bind off loosely. Graft left shoulder. Sew neckband seam.

Finish Sleeves

PU & K 128 (136, 136, 144, 152, 152, 10, 172, 172) sts across sleeve end. Purl 3 rows. Bind off loosely. Rep for other sleeve. Sew sleeve and side seams. Weave in ends.

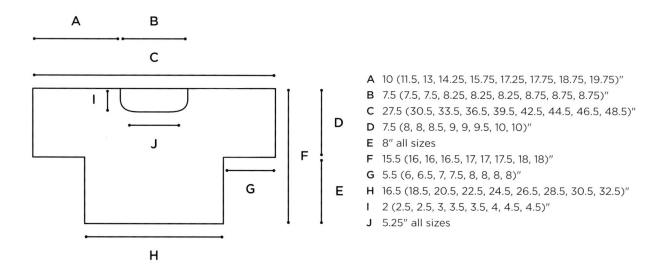

A 10 (11.5, 13, 14.25, 15.75, 17.25, 17.75, 18.75, 19.75)″
B 7.5 (7.5, 7.5, 8.25, 8.25, 8.25, 8.75, 8.75, 8.75)″
C 27.5 (30.5, 33.5, 36.5, 39.5, 42.5, 44.5, 46.5, 48.5)″
D 7.5 (8, 8, 8.5, 9, 9, 9.5, 10, 10)″
E 8″ all sizes
F 15.5 (16, 16, 16.5, 17, 17, 17.5, 18, 18)″
G 5.5 (6, 6.5, 7, 7.5, 8, 8, 8)″
H 16.5 (18.5, 20.5, 22.5, 24.5, 26.5, 28.5, 30.5, 32.5)″
I 2 (2.5, 2.5, 3, 3.5, 3.5, 4, 4.5, 4.5)″
J 5.25″ all sizes

Ripple Lace Stitch Pattern

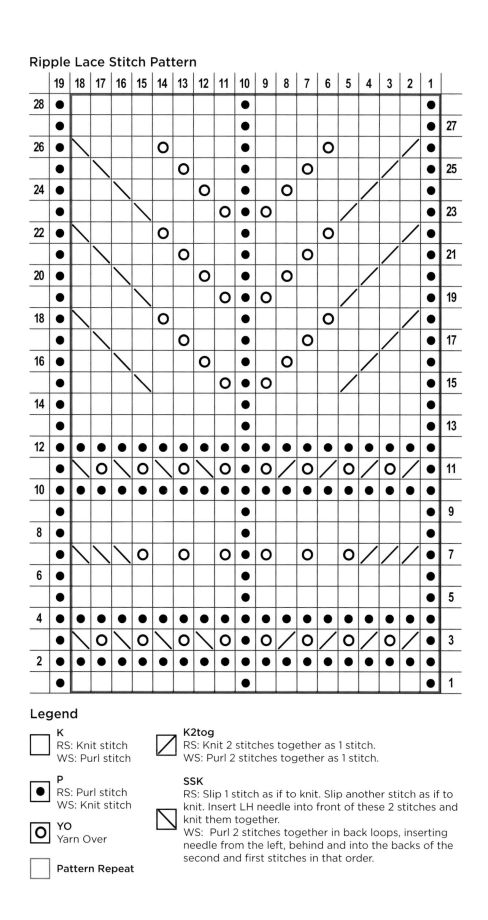

Legend

	K		K2tog
☐	RS: Knit stitch WS: Purl stitch	◿	RS: Knit 2 stitches together as 1 stitch. WS: Purl 2 stitches together as 1 stitch.

K
RS: Knit stitch
WS: Purl stitch

P
RS: Purl stitch
WS: Knit stitch

YO
Yarn Over

Pattern Repeat

K2tog
RS: Knit 2 stitches together as 1 stitch.
WS: Purl 2 stitches together as 1 stitch.

SSK
RS: Slip 1 stitch as if to knit. Slip another stitch as if to knit. Insert LH needle into front of these 2 stitches and knit them together.
WS: Purl 2 stitches together in back loops, inserting needle from the left, behind and into the backs of the second and first stitches in that order.

SALEM SHAWL

by Rebecca L. Minner

FINISHED MEASUREMENTS

44.5" back depth, 89" wide at widest point.

YARN

Knit Picks Alpaca Cloud Fingering
(100% Superfine Alpaca; 200 yards/50g): Oscar 26895, 9 skeins.

NEEDLES

US 5 (3.75mm) 40" circular needles, or size to obtain gauge.

NOTIONS

Yarn Needle
Removable or Locking Stitch Markers
Smooth Scrap Yarn (1 yard, cotton preferred)
Crochet Hook
Thread for a Lifeline (optional)
Blocking Pins or Wires

GAUGE

23 sts and 34.5 rows = 4" in St st, unblocked.

20 sts and 34.5 rows = 4" in St st, blocked.

For pattern support, contact
ampersanddesignsco@gmail.com

Notes:

Wrap yourself in a galaxy of alpaca stars with this generously sized shawl that features an eight pointed star design arranged over a geometric lace pattern that criss-crosses busily in the background. Worked from the top center out to the bottom, it all begins with a provisionally cast on Garter stitch tab and increases along the edges and down the middle to create a triangular shawl without disturbing the fields of lace in between. In lieu of a bind off, a sawtooth edging worked perpendicular to the body of the shawl prevents the lower edge from being bound off too tightly, while forming a decorative border that echoes the right angles found throughout the design.

Both charts and written instructions have been provided. Charts only show RS rows, read them from right to left.

A lifeline on the last WS row before working the edging can be helpful, but is completely optional.

DIRECTIONS

Set Up

The shawl begins with a Garter stitch tab and grows from the center out, increasing 4 sts every RS row.

Cast On

To provisionally CO 2 sts, chain 6 with crochet hook and scrap yarn. Using working yarn, PU 2 sts in bumps on back of chain. Knit 5 rows.

Row 1 (RS): K2, do not turn. Rotate work 90 degrees clockwise and PU 3 sts along edge; one st in each of the garter ridge bumps along edge of work. 5 sts. Rotate 90 degrees again and carefully remove scrap yarn, returning the 2 sts to LH needle, K2. 7 sts total.

Row 2 (WS): K2, P3, K2.
Row 3: K2, (YO, K1) 4 times, K1. 11 sts.
Row 4: K2, P7, K2.
Row 5: K2, (YO, K3, YO, K1) 2 times, K1. 15 sts.
Row 6: K2, P11, K2.

Set Up Instructions

Work from Set Up chart, or follow written instructions. To follow chart, on the RS K2, work across chart, K1, rep row from chart, K2. On WS rows, K2, P to last 2 sts, K2.

Each RS row increases 4 sts.

Row 1 (RS): K2, (YO, K1, K2tog, YO, K2, YO, K1) 2 times. K1.
Row 2 and all even rows (WS): K2, P to last 2 sts, K2.
Row 3: K2, (YO, K1, K2tog, YO, K1, YO, SSK, K1, YO, K1) 2 times, K1.
Row 5: K2, (YO, K1, K2tog, YO, K3, YO, SSK, K1, YO, K1) 2 times, K1.
Row 7: K2, (YO, *K1, K2tog, YO* 2 times, K2, YO, SSK, K1, YO, K1) 2 times, K1.
Row 9: K2, (YO, *K1, K2tog, YO* 2 times, K1, *YO, SSK, K1* 2 times, YO, K1) 2 times, K1.
Row 11: K2, (YO, *K1, K2tog, YO* 2 times, K3, *YO, SSK, K1* 2 times, YO, K1) 2 times, K1.
Row 13: K2, (YO, *K1, K2tog, YO* 3 times, K2, *YO, SSK, K1* 2 times. YO, K1) 2 times, K1.
Row 15: K2, (YO, *K1, K2tog, YO* 3 times, K1, *YO, SSK, K1* 3 times, YO, K1) 2 times, K1.
Row 17: K2, (YO, K4, *K2tog, YO, K1* 2 times, K2, *YO, SSK, K1* 2 times, K3, YO, K1) 2 times, K1.
Row 19: K2, (YO, K4, SSK, YO, *K1, K2tog, YO* 2 times, K2, YO, SSK, K1, YO, K2tog, K4, YO, K1) 2 times, K1.
Row 21: K2, (YO, K1, K2tog, YO, K4, *K2tog, YO, K1* 2 times, *YO, SSK, K1* 2 times, K3, YO, SSK, K1, YO, K1) 2 times, K1.
Row 23: K2, (YO, K1, K2 tog, YO, K7, K2tog, YO, K3, YO, SSK, K7, YO, SSK, K1, YO, K1) 2 times, K1.
Row 25: K2, (YO, K1, K2tog, YO, K7, SSK, YO, K1, K2tog, YO, K2, YO, K2tog, K7, YO, SSK, K1, YO, K1) 2 times, K1.
Row 27: K2, (YO, *K1, K2tog, YO* 2 times, K7, K2tog, YO, K1, YO, SSK, K7, *YO, SSK, K1* 2 times, YO, K1) 2 times, K1.
Row 29: K2, (YO, *K1, K2tog, YO* 2 times, K21, *YO, SSK, K1* 2 times, YO, K1) 2 times, K1.
Row 31: K2, (YO, *K1, K2tog, YO* 2 times, K10, SSK, YO, K11, *YO, SSK, K1* 2 times, YO, K1) 2 times, K1.

Row 33: K2, (YO, *K1, K2tog, YO* 3 times, K19, *YO, SSK, K1* 3 times, YO, K1) 2 times, K1.
Row 35: K2, (YO, K39, YO, K1) 2 times, K1.
Row 37: K2, (YO, K41, YO, K1) 2 times, K1.
Row 39: K2, (YO, K1, K2tog, YO, K37, YO, SSK, K1, YO, K1) 2 times, K1.
Row 41: K2, (YO, *K1, K2tog, YO* 2 times, K33, *YO, SSK, K1* 2 times, YO, K1) 2 times, K1.
Row 43: K2, (YO, *K1, K2tog, YO* 2 times, K35, *YO, SSK, K1* 2 times, YO, K1) 2 times, K1.
Row 45: K2, (YO, *K1, K2tog, YO* 3 times, K31, *YO, SSK, K1* 3 times, YO, K1) 2 times, K1.
Row 47: K2, (YO, *K1, K2tog, YO* 4 times, K27, *YO, SSK, K1* 4 times, YO, K1) 2 times, K1.
Row 49: K2, (YO, *K1, K2tog, YO* 4 times, K29, *YO, SSK, K1* 4 times, YO, K1) 2 times, K1.
Row 51: K2, (YO, *K1, K2tog, YO* 5 times, K25, *YO, SSK, K1* 5 times, YO, K1) 2 times, K1.
Row 53: K2, (YO, *K1, K2tog, YO* 6 times, K21, *YO, SSK, K1* 6 times, YO, K1) 2 times, K1. 123 sts.
Row 54: K2, P to last 2 sts, K2.

Body

The body continues increasing 4 stitches every RS row, as established.

Work from the charts, or the following written instructions. To use charts, on the RS K2, work across Right Edge chart, work across Center chart, and then across Left Edge chart, PM, K1, work across charts again, K2. On WS rows, K2, P to last 2 sts, K2.
Rep charts twice (232 rows), working Center chart 3 times the second time you work them. 355 sts after first chart rep, 587 sts after second.

To follow written instructions, work 116 rows as follows then rep pattern again, this time working section between brackets three times.

The Right Edge, Center, and Left Edge charts are split across two pages.

Row 1 (RS): K2, *YO, [(K1, YO, SSK) 6 times, K23, (K2tog, YO, K1) 5 times, K2tog, YO] K1, YO, PM, K1* rep between ** once more, only PM on first rep to mark center st of shawl, K1. SM on all following rows.
Row 2 and all even rows (WS): K2, P to last 2 sts, K2.
Row 3: K2, *YO, K1, [K1, (K1, YO, SSK) 5 times, K27, (K2tog, YO, K1) 5 times], K2, YO, K1* rep between ** twice, K1.
Row 5: K2, *YO, K1, K2tog, [YO, K2, (YO, SSK, K1) 4 times, YO, K2tog, K25, SSK, (YO, K1, K2tog) 5 times], YO, K2, YO, K1* rep between ** twice, K1.
Row 7: K2, *YO, K1, K2tog, YO, [(K1, YO, SSK) 5 times, K29, (K2tog, YO, K1) 4 times, K2tog, YO], K1, YO, SSK, K1, YO, K1* rep between ** twice, K1.
Row 9: K2, *YO, K1, K2tog, YO, K1, [K1, (K1, YO, SSK) 4 times, K33, (K2tog, YO, K1) 4 times], K2, YO, SSK, K1, YO, K1* rep between ** twice, K1.

Row 11: K2, *(YO, K1, K2tog) 2 times, [YO, K2, (YO, SSK, K1) 3 times, YO, K2tog, K31, SSK, (YO, K1, K2tog) 4 times], YO, K2, YO, SSK, K1, YO, K1* rep between ** twice, K1.

Row 13: K2, *YO, (K1, K2tog, YO) 2 times, [(K1, YO, SSK) 4 times, K35, (K2tog, YO, K1) 3 times, K2tog, YO], (K1, YO, SSK) 2 times, K1, YO, K1* rep between ** twice, K1.

Row 15: K2, *YO, (K1, K2tog, YO) 2 times, K1, [K1, (K1, YO, SSK) 3 times, K39, (K2tog, YO, K1) 3 times], K2, (YO, SSK, K1) 2 times, YO, K1* rep between ** twice, K1.

Row 17: K2, *(YO, K1, K2tog) 3 times, [YO, K2, (YO, SSK, K1) 2 times, YO, K2tog, K37, SSK, (YO, K1, K2tog) 3 times], YO, K2, (YO, SSK, K1) 2 times, YO, K1* rep between ** twice, K1.

Row 19: K2, *YO, (K1, K2tog, YO) 3 times, [(K1, YO, SSK) 6 times, K1, YO, K2tog, K17, SSK, YO, (K1, K2tog, YO) 6 times], (K1, YO, SSK) 3 times, K1, YO, K1* rep between ** twice, K1.

Row 21: K2, *YO, K4, (K2tog, YO, K1) 2 times, [K1, (K1, YO, SSK) 2 times, K4, (YO, SSK, K1) 2 times, YO, SSK, K10, YO, SSK, K9, (K2tog, YO, K1) 2 times, K2tog, YO, K4, (K2tog, YO, K1) 2 times], K1, (K1, YO, SSK) 2 times, K4, YO, K1* rep between ** twice, K1.

Row 23: K2, *YO, K4, SSK, (YO, K1, K2tog) 2 times, [YO, K2, YO, SSK, K1, YO, K2tog, K3, (K1, YO, SSK) 3 times, K19, (K2tog, YO, K1) 3 times, K3, SSK, (YO, K1, K2tog) 2 times], YO, K2, YO, SSK, K1, YO, K2tog, K4, YO, K1* rep between ** twice, K1.

Row 25: K2, *YO, K1, K2tog, YO, K3, (K1, K2tog, YO) 2 times, [(K1, YO, SSK) 2 times, K4, (YO, SSK, K1) 3 times, YO, K2tog, K7, YO, SK2P, YO, K7, SSK, (YO, K1, K2tog) 3 times YO, K3, (K1, K2tog, YO) 2 times], (K1, YO, SSK) 2 times, K4, YO, SSK, K1, YO, K1* rep between ** twice, K1.

Row 27: K2, *YO, K1, K2tog, YO, K7, K2tog, YO, K1, [K2, YO, SSK, K7, (YO, SSK, K1) 3 times, K6, YO, SSK, SSK, YO, K1, K2tog, YO, K7, (K2tog, YO, K1) 3 times, K6, K2tog, YO, K1], K2, YO, SSK, K7, YO, SSK, K1, YO, K1* rep between ** twice, K1.

Row 29: K2, *YO, K1, K2tog, YO, K7, SSK, YO, K1, K2tog, [YO, K2, YO, K2tog, K7, (YO, SSK, K1) 3 times, K6, YO, SSK, K1, K2tog, YO, K7, (K2tog, YO, K1) 3 times, K6, SSK, YO, K1, K2tog], YO, K2, YO, K2tog, K7, YO, SSK, K1, YO, K1* rep between ** twice, K1.

Row 31: K2, *(YO, K1, K2tog) 2 times, YO, K7, K2tog, YO, [K1, YO, SSK, K7, (YO, SSK, K1) 3 times, YO, K2tog, K4, YO, SSK, K1, YO, SK2P, YO, K1, K2tog, YO, K4, SSK, YO, (K1, K2tog, YO) 3 times, K7, K2tog, YO], K1, YO, SSK, K7, (YO, SSK, K1) 2 times, YO, K1* rep between ** twice, K1.

Row 33: K2, *(YO, K1, K2tog) 2 times, YO, K10, [K11, (YO, SSK, K1) 3 times, K2, (K1, YO, SSK) 2 times, SSK, YO, (K1, K2tog, YO) 2 times, K4, (K2tog, YO, K1) 3 times, K9], K11, (YO, SSK, K1) 2 times, YO, K1* repeat between ** twice, K1.

Row 35: K2, *(YO, K1, K2tog) 2 times, YO, K10, SSK, [YO, K11, (YO, SSK, K1) 3 times, K3, (YO, SSK, K1) 2 times, (K2tog, YO, K1) 2 times, K3, (K2tog, YO, K1) 3 times, K9, SSK], YO, K11, (YO, SSK, K1) 2 times, YO, K1* rep between ** twice, K1.

Row 37: K2, *YO, (K1, K2tog, YO) 3 times, K9, [K10, (YO, SSK, K1) 3 times, YO, K2tog, (K1, YO, SSK) 2 times, K1, YO, SK2P, (YO, K1, K2tog) 2 times, YO, K1, SSK, (YO, K1, K2tog) 3 times, YO, K9], K10, (YO, SSK, K1) 3 times, YO, K1* rep between ** twice, K1.

Row 39: K2, *YO, K19, [K20, (YO, SSK, K1) 2 times, YO, SSK, SSK, YO, (K1, K2tog, YO) 3 times, K19], K20, YO, K1* rep between ** twice, K1.

Row 41: K2, *YO, K20, [K21, (YO, SSK, K1) 3 times, (K2tog, YO, K1) 3 times, K19], K21, YO, K1* rep between ** twice, K1.

Row 43: K2, *YO, K1, K2tog, YO, K18, [K19, (YO, SSK, K1) 3 times, YO, SK2P, (YO, K1, K2tog) 3 times, YO, K18], K19, YO, SSK, K1, YO, K1* rep between ** twice, K1.

Row 45: K2, *(YO, K1, K2tog) 2 times, YO, K16, [K17, (YO, SSK, K1) 3 times, YO, SSK, SSK, (YO, K1, K2tog) 4 times, YO, K16], K17, (YO, SSK, K1) 2 times, YO, K1* rep between ** twice, K1.

Row 47: K2, *(YO, K1, K2tog) 2 times, YO, K17, [K18, (YO, SSK, K1) 4 times, (K2tog, YO, K1) 4 times, K16], K18, (YO, SSK, K1) 2 times, YO, K1* rep between ** twice, K1.

Row 49: K2, *(YO, K1, K2tog) 3 times, YO, K15, [K16, (YO, SSK, K1) 4 times, YO, SK2P, (YO, K1, K2tog) 4 times, YO, K15], K16, (YO, SSK, K1) 3 times, YO, K1* rep between ** twice, K1.

Row 51: K2, *(YO, K1, K2tog) 4 times, YO, K13, [K14, (YO, SSK, K1) 4 times, YO, SSK, SSK, (YO, K1, K2tog) 5 times, YO, K13], K14, (YO, SSK, K1) 4 times, YO, K1* rep between ** twice, K1.

Row 53: K2, *(YO, K1, K2tog) 4 times, YO, K14, [K15, (YO, SSK, K1) 5 times, (K2tog, YO, K1) 5 times, K13], K15, (YO, SSK, K1) 4 times, YO, K1* rep between ** twice, K1.

Row 55: K2, *(YO, K1, K2tog) 5 times, YO, K12, [K13, (YO, SSK, K1) 5 times, YO, SK2P, (YO, K1, K2tog) 5 times, YO, K12], K13, (YO, SSK, K1) 5 times, YO, K1* rep between ** twice, K1.

Row 57: K2, *(YO, K1, K2tog) 6 times, YO, K10, [K11, (YO, SSK, K1) 5 times, YO, SSK, SSK, (YO, K1, K2tog) 6 times, YO, K10], K11, (YO, SSK, K1) 6 times, YO, K1* rep between ** twice, K1.

Row 59: K2, *YO, (K1, YO, SSK) 6 times, K11, [K12, (K2tog, YO, K1) 6 times, (YO, SSK, K1) 6 times, K10], K12, (K2tog, YO, K1) 6 times, YO, K1* rep between ** twice, K1.

Row 61: K2, *YO, K3, (YO, SSK, K1) 5 times, K12, [K14, (K2tog, YO, K1) 5 times, K1, (K1, YO, SSK) 5 times, K13], K14, (K2tog, YO, K1) 5 times, K2, YO, K1* rep between ** twice, K1.

Row 63: K2, *YO, K1, K2tog, YO, K2, (YO, SSK, K1) 4 times, YO, K2tog, K12, [K13, SSK, YO, (K1, K2tog, YO) 5 times, K2, YO, (SSK, K1, YO) 4 times, K2tog, K12], K13, SSK, YO, (K1, K2tog, YO) 5 times, K2, YO* rep between ** twice, K1.

Row 65: K2, *YO, K1, K2tog, YO, (K1, YO, SSK) 5 times, K14, [K15, (K2tog, YO, K1) 5 times, (YO, SSK, K1) 5 times, K13], K15, (K2tog, YO, K1) 5 times, YO, SSK, K1, YO, K1* rep between ** twice, K1.

Row 67: K2, *YO, K1, K2tog, YO, K3, (YO, SSK, K1) 4 times, K15, [K17, (K2tog, YO, K1) 4 times, K1, (K1, YO, SSK) 4 times, K16], K17, (K2tog, YO, K1) 4 times, K2, YO, SSK, K1, YO, K1* rep between ** twice, K1.

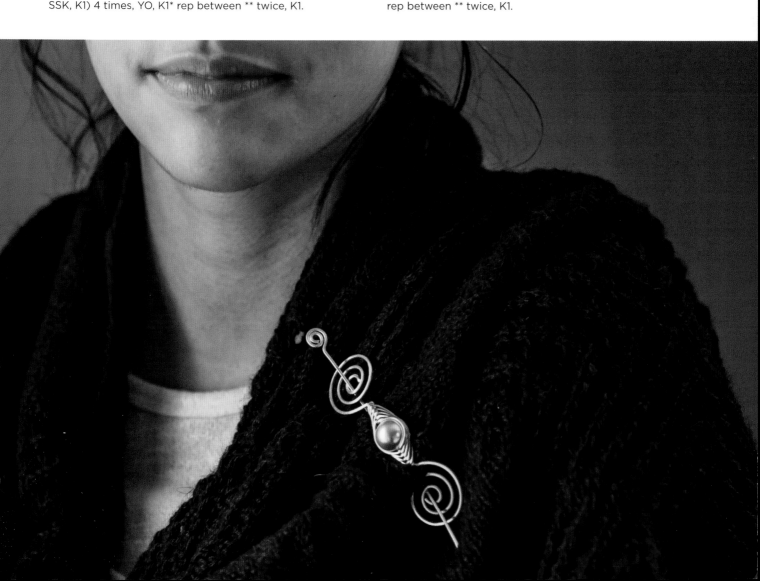

Row 69: K2, *YO, (K1, K2tog, YO) 2 times, K2, (YO, SSK, K1) 3 times, YO, K2tog, K15, [K16, SSK, YO, (K1, K2tog, YO) 4 times, K2, (YO, SSK, K1) 3 times, YO, K2tog, K15], K16, SSK, YO, (K1, K2tog, YO) 4 times, K2, YO, SSK, K1, YO, K1* rep between ** twice, K1.

Row 71: K2, *YO, (K1, K2tog, YO) 2 times, (K1, YO, SSK) 4 times, K17, [K18, (K2tog, YO, K1) 4 times, (YO, SSK, K1) 4 times, K16], K18, (K2tog, YO, K1) 4 times, (YO, SSK, K1) 2 times, YO, K1* rep between ** twice, K1.

Row 73: K2, *YO, (K1, K2tog, YO) 2 times, K2, (K1, YO, SSK) 3 times, K19, [K20, (K2tog, YO, K1) 3 times, K1, (K1, YO, SSK) 3 times, K19], K20, (K2tog, YO, K1) 3 times, K1, (K1, YO, SSK) 2 times, K1, YO, K1* rep between ** twice, K1.

Row 75: K2, *YO, (K1, K2tog, YO) 3 times, K2, (YO, SSK, K1) 2 times, YO, K2tog, K18, [K19, SSK, YO, K1, (K2tog, YO, K1) 3 times, (K1, YO, SSK) 2 times, K1, YO, K2tog, K18], K19, SSK, YO, K1, (K2tog, YO, K1) 3 times, (K1, YO, SSK) 2 times, K1, YO, K1* rep between ** twice, K1.

Row 77: K2, *YO, K1, (K2tog, YO, K1) 3 times, (YO, SSK, K1) 6 times, YO, K2tog, K8, [K9, SSK, YO, (K1, K2tog, YO) 6 times, K1, (YO, SSK, K1) 6 times, YO, K2tog, K8], K9, SSK, YO, (K1, K2tog, YO) 6 times, K1, (YO, SSK, K1) 3 times, YO, K1* rep between ** twice, K1.

Row 79: K2, *YO, K4, (K2tog, YO, K1) 2 times, K1, (K1, YO, SSK) 2 times, K4, (YO, SSK, K1) 3 times, K9, [YO, SSK, K9, (K2tog, YO, K1) 3 times, K3, (K2tog, YO, K1) 2 times, K1, (K1, YO, SSK) 2 times, K4, (YO, SSK, K1) 3 times, K9], YO, SSK, K9, (K2tog, YO, K1) 3 times, K3, (K2tog, YO, K1) 2 times, K1, (K1, YO, SSK) 2 times, K4, YO, K1* rep between ** twice, K1.

Row 81: K2, *YO, K4, SSK, YO, (K1, K2tog, YO) 2 times, K2, YO, SSK, K1, YO, K2tog, K4, (YO, SSK, K1) 3 times, K8, [K10, (K2tog, YO, K1) 3 times, K3, SSK, YO, (K1, K2tog, YO) 2 times, K2, YO, SSK, K1, YO, K2tog, K4, (YO, SSK, K1) 3 times, K8], K10, (K2tog, YO, K1) 3 times, K3, SSK, YO, (K1, K2tog, YO) 2 times, K2, YO, SSK, K1, YO, K2tog, K4, YO, K1* rep between ** twice, K1.

Row 83: K2, *YO, K1, K2tog, YO, K4, (K2tog, YO, K1) 2 times, (YO, SSK, K1) 2 times, K3, (YO, SSK, K1) 3 times, YO, K2tog, K7, YO, [SK2P, YO, K7, SSK, YO, (K1, K2tog, YO) 3 times, K4, (K2tog, YO, K1) 2 times, (YO, SSK, K1) 2 times, K3, (YO, SSK, K1) 3 times, YO, K2tog, K7, YO], SK2P, YO, K7, SSK, YO, (K1, K2tog, YO) 3 times, K4, (K2tog, YO, K1) 2 times, (YO, SSK, K1) 2 times, K3, YO, SSK, K1, YO, K1* rep between ** twice, K1.

Row 85: K2, *YO, K1, K2tog, YO, K7, K2tog, YO, K3, YO, SSK, K7, (YO, SSK, K1) 3 times, K6, YO, SSK, SSK, [YO, K1, K2tog, YO, K7, (K2tog, YO, K1) 3 times, K6, K2tog, YO, K3, YO, SSK, K7, (YO, SSK, K1) 3 times, K6, YO, SSK, SSK], YO, K1, K2tog, YO, K7, (K2tog, YO, K1) 3 times, K6, K2tog, YO, K3, YO, SSK, K7, YO, SSK, K1, YO, K1* rep between ** twice, K1.

Row 87: K2, *YO, K1, K2tog, YO, K7, SSK, YO, K1, K2tog, YO, K2, YO, K2tog, K7, (YO, SSK, K1) 3 times, K6, YO, SSK, [K1, K2tog, YO, K7, (K2tog, YO, K1) 3 times, K6, SSK, YO, K1, K2tog, YO, K2, YO, K2tog, K7, (YO, SSK, K1) 3 times, K6, YO, SSK], K1, K2tog, YO, K7, (K2tog, YO, K1) 3 times, K6, SSK, YO, K1, K2tog, YO, K2, YO, K2tog, K7, (YO, SSK, K1, YO, K1* rep between ** twice, K1.

Row 89: K2, *YO, (K1, K2tog, YO) 2 times, K7, K2tog, YO, K1, YO, SSK, K7, (YO, SSK, K1) 3 times, YO, K2tog, K4, YO, SSK, K1, YO, [SK2P, YO, K1, K2tog, YO, K4, SSK, YO, (K1, K2tog, YO) 3 times, K7, K2tog, YO, K1, YO, SSK, K7, (YO, SSK, K1) 3 times, YO, K2tog, K4, YO, SSK, K1, YO], SK2P, YO, K1, K2tog, YO, K4, SSK, YO, (K1, K2tog, YO) 3 times, K7, K2tog, YO, K1, YO, SSK, K7, (YO, SSK, K1) 2 times, YO, K1* rep between ** twice, K1.

Row 91: K2, *YO, (K1, K2tog, YO) 2 times, K21, (YO, SSK, K1) 3 times, K3, YO, SSK, K1, YO, SSK, SSK, [YO, (K1, K2tog, YO) 2 times, K4, (K2tog, YO, K1) 3 times, K20, (YO, SSK, K1) 3 times, K3, YO, SSK, K1, YO, SSK, SSK], YO, (K1, K2tog, YO) 2 times, K4, (K2tog, YO, K1) 3 times, K20, (YO, SSK, K1) 2 times, YO, K1* rep between ** twice, K1.

Row 93: K2, *YO, (K1, K2tog, YO) 2 times, K10, SSK, YO, K11, (YO, SSK, K1) 3 times, K3, YO, SSK, K1, YO, SSK, [(K1, K2tog, YO) 2 times, K4, (K2tog, YO, K1) 3 times, K9, SSK, YO, K11, (YO, SSK, K1) 3 times, K3, YO, SSK, K1, YO, SSK], (K1, K2tog, YO) 2 times, K4, (K2tog, YO, K1) 3 times, K9, SSK, YO, K11, (YO, SSK, K1) 2 times, YO, K1* rep between ** twice, K1.

Row 95: K2, *YO, (K1, K2tog, YO) 3 times, K19, (YO, SSK, K1) 3 times, YO, K2tog, (K1, YO, SSK) 2 times, K1, YO, [SK2P, YO, (K1, K2tog, YO) 2 times, K1, SSK, YO, (K1, K2tog, YO) 3 times, K19, (YO, SSK, K1) 3 times, YO, K2tog, (K1, YO, SSK) 2 times, K1, YO], SK2P, YO, (K1, K2tog, YO) 2 times, K1, SSK, YO, (K1, K2tog, YO) 3 times, K19, (YO, SSK, K1) 3 times, YO, K1* rep between ** twice, K1.

Row 97: K2, *YO, K39, (YO, SSK, K1) 2 times, YO, SSK, SSK, [(YO, K1, K2tog) 3 times, YO, K39, (YO, SSK, K1) 2 times, YO, SSK, SSK], (YO, K1, K2tog) 3 times, YO, K39, YO, K1* rep between ** twice, K1.

Row 99: K2, *YO, K41, (YO, SSK, K1) 2 times, YO, SSK, [(K1, K2tog, YO) 3 times, K41, (YO, SSK, K1) 2 times, YO, SSK], (K1, K2tog, YO) 3 times, K41, YO, K1* rep between ** twice, K1.

Row 101: K2, *YO, K1, K2tog, YO, K37, (YO, SSK, K1) 3 times, YO, [SK2P, YO, (K1, K2tog, YO) 3 times, K37, (YO, SSK, K1) 3 times, YO], SK2P, YO, (K1, K2tog, YO) 3 times, K37, YO, SSK, K1, YO, K1* rep between ** twice, K1.

Row 103: K2, *YO, (K1, K2tog, YO) 2 times, K33, (YO, SSK, K1) 3 times, YO, SSK, SSK, [YO, (K1, K2tog, YO) 4 times, K33, (YO, SSK, K1) 3 times, YO, SSK, SSK], YO, (K1, K2tog, YO) 4 times, K33, (YO, SSK, K1) 2 times, YO, K1* rep between ** twice, K1.

Row 105: K2, *YO, (K1, K2tog, YO) 2 times, K35, (YO, SSK, K1) 3 times, YO, SSK, [(K1, K2tog, YO) 4 times, K35, (YO, SSK, K1) 3 times, YO, SSK], (K1, K2tog, YO) 4 times, K35, (YO, SSK, K1) 2 times, YO, K1* rep between ** twice, K1.

Row 107: K2, *YO, (K1, K2tog, YO) 3 times, K31, (YO, SSK, K1) 4 times, YO, [SK2P, YO, (K1, K2tog, YO) 4 times, K31, (YO, SSK, K1) 4 times, YO], SK2P, YO, (K1, K2tog, YO) 4 times, K31, (YO, SSK, K1) 3 times, YO, K1* rep between ** twice, K1.

Row 109: K2, *YO, (K1, K2tog, YO) 4 times, K27, (YO, SSK, K1) 4 times, YO, SSK, SSK, [YO, (K1, K2tog, YO) 5 times, K27, (YO, SSK, K1) 4 times, YO, SSK, SSK], YO, (K1, K2tog, YO) 5 times, K27, (YO, SSK, K1) 4 times, YO, K1* rep between ** twice, K1.

Row 111: K2, *YO, (K1, K2tog, YO) 4 times, K29, (YO, SSK, K1) 4 times, YO, SSK, [(K1, K2tog, YO) 5 times, K29, (YO, SSK, K1) 4 times, YO, SSK], (K1, K2tog, YO) 5 times, K29, (YO, SSK, K1) 4 times, YO, K1* rep between ** twice, K1.

Row 113: K2, *YO, (K1, K2tog, YO) 5 times, K25, (YO, SSK, K1) 5 times, YO, [SK2P, YO, (K1, K2tog, YO) 5 times, K25, (YO, SSK, K1) 5 times, YO], SK2P, YO, (K1, K2tog, YO) 5 times, K25, (YO, SSK, K1) 5 times, YO, K1* rep between ** twice, K1.

Row 115: K2, *YO, (K1, K2tog, YO) 6 times, K21, (YO, SSK, K1) 5 times, YO, SSK, SSK, [YO, (K1, K2tog, YO) 6 times, K21, (YO, SSK, K1) 5 times, YO, SSK, SSK], YO, (K1, K2tog, YO) 6 times, K21, (YO, SSK, K1) 6 times, YO, K1* rep between ** twice, K1.

Row 116: K2, P to last 2 sts, K2.

Edging

Instead of a BO, a pointed Garter stitch edging is worked sideways, decreasing one st every other row. At the point of the shawl, sts are BO slightly differently to avoid any puckers or pulling.

Edging Instructions

With RS facing, CO 2 sts onto LH needle next to Body sts.

Row 1 (RS): K1, K2tog (1 st just CO and 1 st from Body), turn.
Row 2 (WS): Move yarn to back, K1, YO, K1.
Row 3: K1, K1 TBL to twist YO closed, K2tog, turn.
Rows 4, 6, 8, 10, 12, 14: Move yarn to back, K to last st, YO, K1.
Row 5: K1, K1 TBL, K1, K2tog, turn.
Row 7: K1, K1 TBL, K2, K2tog, turn.
Row 9: K1, K1 TBL, K3, K2tog, turn.
Row 11: K1, K1 TBL, K4, K2tog, turn.
Row 13: K1, K1 TBL, K5, K2tog, turn.
Row 15: K1, K1 TBL, K6, K2tog, turn.
Rows 16, 18, 20, 22, 24, 26, 28: Move yarn to back, K.
Row 17: K1, SSK, K5, K2tog, turn.

Row 19: K1, SSK, K4, K2tog, turn.
Row 21: K1, SSK, K3, K2tog, turn.
Row 23: K1, SSK, K2, K2tog, turn.
Row 25: K1, SSK, K1, K2tog, turn.
Row 27: K1, SSK, K2tog, turn.
Row 29: K1, Sk2p, turn.
Row 30: Move yarn to back, K1, YO, K1, turn.

Rep Rows 3-30 19 more times.
Work Rows 3-24 once more.

Edging Instructions for Center Point Only

Row 1: K1, SSK, K1, K2tog, insert left needle through st you just BO from back to front (the stitch from the shawl's body that you just BO with a K2tog), turn.
Row 2: Move yarn to back, K.
Row 3: K1, SSK, K2tog (one st being the st you BO and put back on the left needle), turn.
Row 4: Move yarn to back, K.
Row 5: K1, SK2P, turn. (This is the center st of the shawl.)
Row 6: Move yarn to back, K1, YO, K1, turn.
Row 7: K1, K1 TBL, K2tog, insert left needle through st you just BO from back to front (the st from the shawl's body that you just BO with a K2tog), turn.
Row 8: Move yarn to back, K to last stitch, YO, K1.
Row 9: K1, K1 TBL, K1, K2tog (one st being the st you BO and put back on the left needle), turn.
Row 10: Move yarn to back, K to last st, YO, K1.

Work Rows 7-30 of Edging Instructions, then rep Rows 3-30 20 times, omitting YO from Row 30 in final repeat.
BO 2 remaining sts.

Finishing

Weave in ends, wash and block to Finished Measurements.

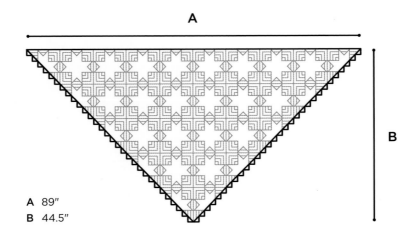

A 89″
B 44.5″

Set Up Chart

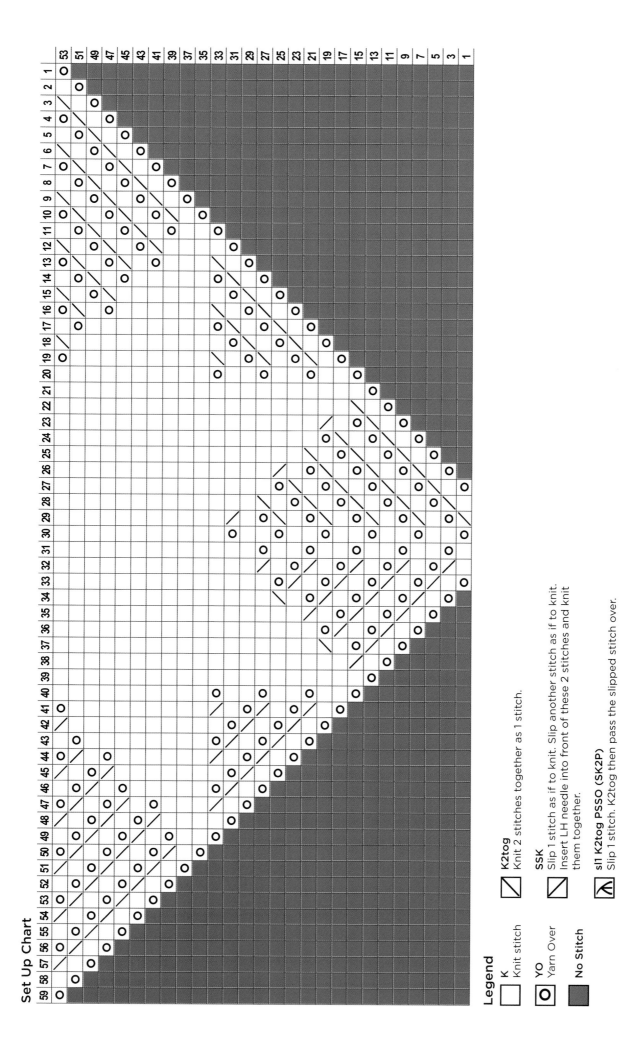

Legend

K
Knit stitch

YO
Yarn Over

No Stitch

K2tog
Knit 2 stitches together as 1 stitch.

SSK
Slip 1 stitch as if to knit. Slip another stitch as if to knit.
Insert LH needle into front of these 2 stitches and knit
them together.

sl1 K2tog PSSO (SK2P)
Slip 1 stitch. K2tog then pass the slipped stitch over.

Right Edge Chart

	115	113	111	109	107	105	103	101	99	97	95	93	91	89	87	85	83
1	O																
2		O															
3	/		O														
4	O	/		O													
5		O	/		O												
6			O	/		O											
7	/			O	/		O										
8	O	/			O	/		O									
9		O	/			O	/		O								
10	O		O	/			O	/		O							
11		O		O	/			O	/		O						
12	/		O		O	/			O	/		O					
13	O	/		O		O	/			O	/		O				
14		O	/		O		O	/			O	/		O			
15	/		O	/		O		O	/			O	/		O		
16	O	/		O	/		O		O	/			O	/		O	
17		O	/		O	/		O		O	/			O	/		O
18	/								O		O	/			O	/	
19	O									O		O	/			O	/
20											O		O	/			O
21																	
22																	
23																	
24																	
25													/				
26														/		O	
27														O	/		O
28													/		O	/	
29											/		O		O	/	
30											O	/		O		O	
31												O	/		O		O
32													O	/		O	/
33													O	/		O	
34															/		O
35																/	
36																	
37																	
38																	
39																	
40							O			O			O				O
41	O										/		O	/		O	/
42	/		O							/		O	/		O	/	
43	O	/		O						O	/		O	/		O	/
44	/		O	/		O					O	/		O	/		O
45	O	/		O	/		O				O	/		O	/		O
46		O	/		O	/		O				O	/		O	/	O
47	O	/		O	/		O	/		O			O	/		O	/
48	/		O	/		O	/		O	/			O	/		O	/
49	O	/		O	/		O	/		O		O	/		O	/	
50	O	/		O	/		O	/		O	/		O	/		O	
51	/		O	/		O	/		O	/		O	/		O	/	
52	O	/		O	/		O	/		O	/		O	/			
53	O	/		O	/		O	/		O	/		O		O		
54		O	/		O	/		O	/		O	/		O			
55		O	/		O	/		O	/		O	/		O		O	
56		O	/		O	/		O	/		O	/			O		
57	/		O	/		O	/		O	/		O	/		O	/	O
58	/	O	/	O		O	/	/	O	/	/	O	/	O	/	/	O

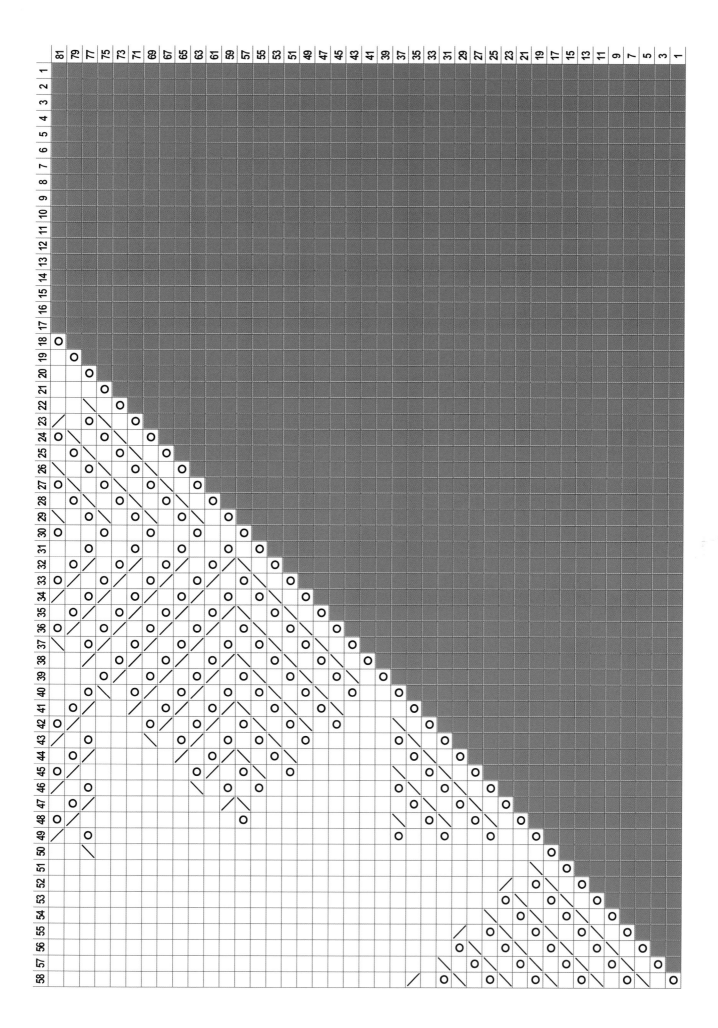

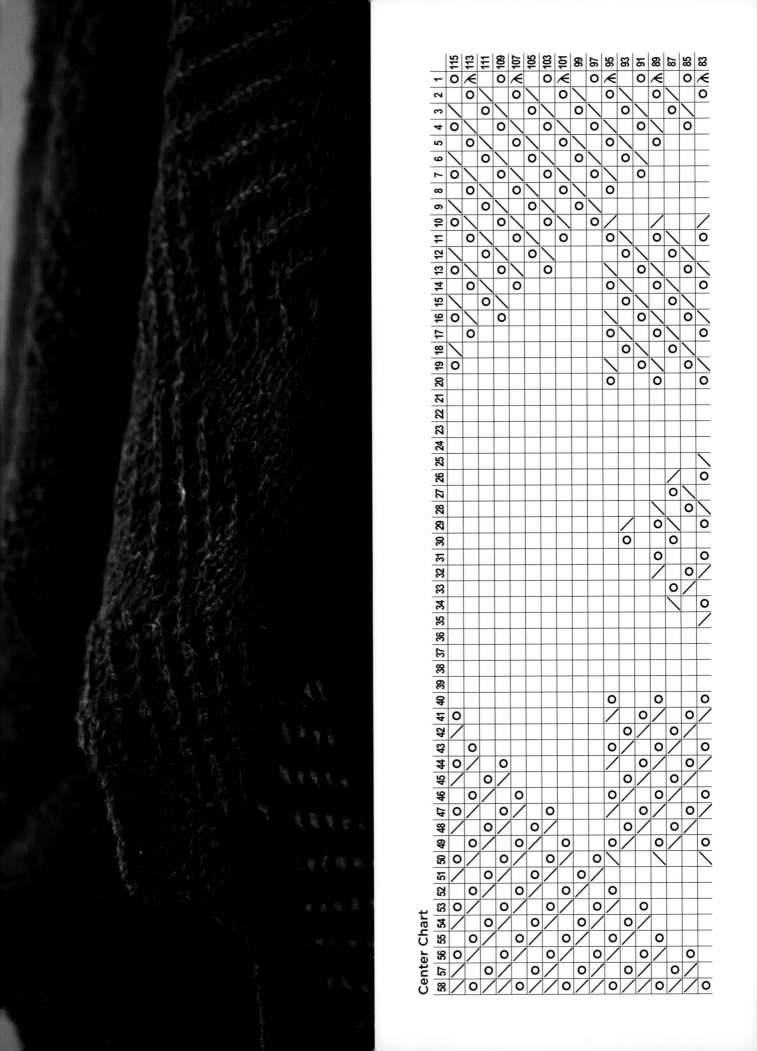

Center Chart

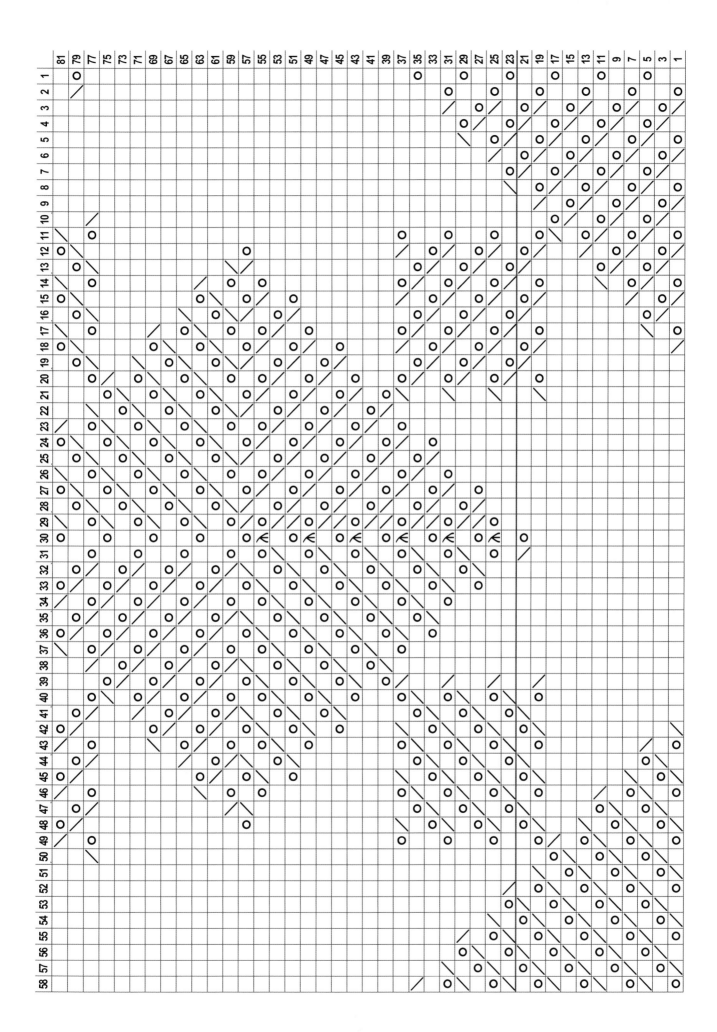

Left Edge Chart

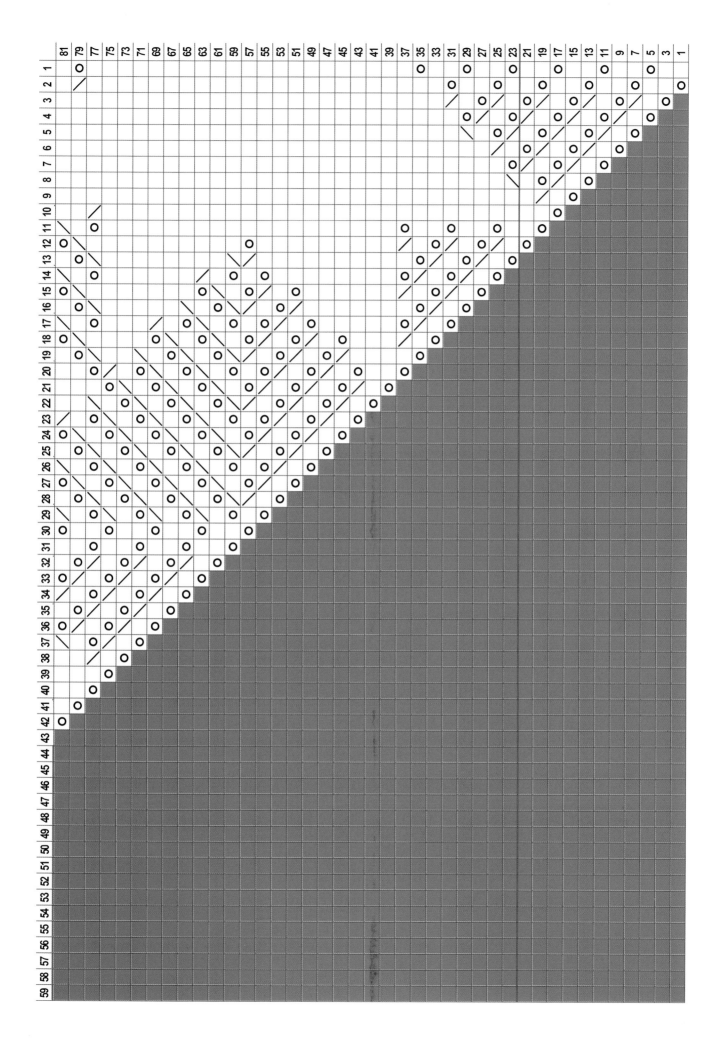

Abbreviations

BO	bind off	**KFB**	knit into the front and back of stitch	**PU**	pick up	**SSP**	sl, sl, p these 2 sts tog tbl
BOR	beginning of round	**K-wise**	knitwise	**P-wise**	purlwise	**SSSK**	sl, sl, sl, k these 3 sts tog
cn	cable needle	**LH**	left hand	**rep**	repeat		
CC	contrast color	**M**	marker	**Rev St st**	reverse stockinette stitch	**St st**	stockinette stitch
CDD	Centered double dec	**M1**	make one stitch	**RH**	right hand	**sts**	stitch(es)
CO	cast on	**M1L**	make one left-leaning stitch	**rnd(s)**	round(s)	**TBL**	through back loop
cont	continue	**M1R**	make one right-leaning stitch	**RS**	right side	**TFL**	through front loop
dec	decrease(es)			**Sk**	skip	**tog**	together
DPN(s)	double pointed needle(s)	**MC**	main color	**Sk2p**	sl 1, k2tog, pass slipped stitch over k2tog: 2 sts dec	**W&T**	wrap & turn (see specific instructions in pattern)
EOR	every other row	**P**	purl				
inc	increase	**P2tog**	purl 2 sts together	**SKP**	sl, k, psso: 1 st dec	**WE**	work even
K	knit	**PM**	place marker	**SL**	slip	**WS**	wrong side
K2tog	knit two sts together	**PFB**	purl into the front and back of stitch	**SM**	slip marker	**WYIB**	with yarn in back
		PSSO	pass slipped stitch over	**SSK**	sl, sl, k these 2 sts tog	**WYIF**	with yarn in front
						YO	yarn over

Knit Picks yarn is both luxe and affordable—a seeming contradiction trounced! But it's not just about the pretty colors; we also care deeply about fiber quality and fair labor practices, leaving you with a gorgeously reliable product you'll turn to time and time again.

THIS COLLECTION FEATURES

Alpaca Cloud
Lace Weight
100% Baby Alpaca

Alpaca Cloud
Fingering Weight
100% Superfine Alpaca

Palette
Fingering Weight
100% Peruvian Highland Wool

Shadow
Lace Weight
100% Merino Wool

Capretta
Fingering Weight
80% Fine Merino Wool,
10% Cashmere, 10% Nylon

Luminance
Hand Painted
Lace Weight
100% Silk

Gloss
Fingering Weight
70% Merino Wool,
30% Silk

Shimmer
Lace Weight
70% Baby Alpaca,
30% Silk

Aloft
Lace Weight
72% Super Kid Mohair,
28% Silk

View these beautiful yarns and more at www.Knit Picks.com